James Waddell Tupper

Tropes and Figures in Anglo-Saxon Prose

James Waddell Tupper

Tropes and Figures in Anglo-Saxon Prose

ISBN/EAN: 9783337416911

Printed in Europe, USA, Canada, Australia, Japan

Cover: Foto ©Thomas Meinert / pixelio.de

More available books at **www.hansebooks.com**

TROPES AND FIGURES

IN

ANGLO-SAXON PROSE

A DISSERTATION

PRESENTED TO THE BOARD OF UNIVERSITY STUDIES OF
THE JOHNS HOPKINS UNIVERSITY FOR THE
DEGREE OF DOCTOR OF PHILOSOPHY

BY

JAMES WADDELL TUPPER

BALTIMORE
JOHN MURPHY & CO.
1897

CONTENTS.

3

TROPES AND FIGURES IN ANGLO-SAXON PROSE.

A precise knowledge of the tropes and figures, found in the literature of any given period, is necessary to a just appreciation of an author's style and of the literary development of his time. The subject may be investigated simply from the point of view of tropes and figures as instruments of literary expression, quite independently of the author or the period ; or as a means by which, on the one hand, the author makes his thought forcible or beautiful, and by which, on the other, the national trend of thought is indicated,—as, here, the peculiar product of the individual, and, there, the common property of the period.

The ancient rhetoricians treated the subject in its relation to the whole body of classical writings without any special reference to individual authors. They regarded it as a branch of Rhetoric, not as a basis for the determination of the author's literary art. Gerber's work[1] is the best modern treatise in the classical method. In it, no investigation is attempted of the styles of the various authors; citations are made from several languages simply as illustrations of tropes and figures.

The numerous monographs which deal with this subject in the classical authors are written mostly from the point of view of individual characteristics of thought and style, and have thereby rendered valuable service to the higher criticism of the texts. The figures of speech and the texts are, necessarily, limited for each monograph.

In Anglo-Saxon only certain figures of speech have been considered, and these only as they occur in poetry. Professor

[1] Gustav Gerber: *Die Sprache als Kunst;* Berlin, 1885. 2 vols.

1

Heinzel's essay [1] on the style of old Germanic poetry called forth Professor Gummere's dissertation [2] on the Anglo-Saxon Metaphor. Prof. Heinzel attempts to show that certain devices were common to all Germanic literature. Such are the epithet, used for the more ordinary pronoun, appositions intended as ornament or explanation, separated from the words to which they refer, the pronoun preceding its noun, variation by means of repetition and parallelism, and the changed succession of words. Then of tropes he finds similes, kennings, and "sensual expressions." The theory advanced by Heinzel to account for the lack of the simile in A. S. as a loss from the primitive Germanic, due to the influence of Romanism and Christianity, is met by Prof. Gummere's theory that the Norse developed the simile of itself, and that the simile did not belong to the parent Germanic stock. The passionate nature of the Germanic race is opposed to the use and development of the simile.

Prof. Gummere then proceeds to an examination of the metaphor in A. S. poetry, and groups his examples in the relations of the concrete and the abstract. As the result of his investigations, he comes to the following conclusion : [3] "The typical A. S. metaphor was originally confined to one word, or, at the farthest, to several words that stood in the closest syntactical relation. This general type has been invaded by the influence of the Latin literature of the Church, especially by the hymns; the result, whether as extended metaphor, simile, or learned allegory, is found not so much in Beowulf as in the Caedmon poems, but even there to no overwhelming extent."

Dr. W. Bode [4] has treated the kenning in detail, and has grouped his full lists of examples in relation to their signification, not as characterizing separate works.

The object of this monograph is to treat with special care the homilies of Ælfric, Wulfstan, and the Blickling Collection, and

[1] Richard Heinzel: Über den Stil der altgermanischen Poesie; *Q. und F.*, X; Strassburg, 1875.

[2] Francis B. Gummere: *The Anglo-Saxon Metaphor;* Halle, 1881.   [3] p. 53.

[4] W. Bode: *Die Kenningar in der Angelsächsischen Dichtung;* Darmstadt und Leipzig, 1886.

the translation of the *Consolation* of *Philosophy* of Boethius, in relation to certain tropes and figures; to show to what extent the original prose of Anglo-Saxon possesses these rhetorical devices, wherein the translation differs from its original, and in what degree the several writers differ from one another; to discover from what spheres of life the tropes are taken, and to judge from that of the intellectual attainments of their authors; to find out, where possible, what figurative ideas are original, and what borrowed; to contrast, where pertinent, the characteristics of prose and poetry in this respect; to establish the degree of excellence which these writers attained in the employment of their instrument, with special reference to the word-figures; and, finally, to form a general estimate of the literary value of these tropes and figures in the monuments considered.

The editions of the texts used are as follows:

The Homilies of the Anglo-Saxon Church:
ed. by B. Thorpe; London, 1844 and
1846. 2 vols.................................A. H., A. H. II.

Wulfstan: herausg. von A. Napier; Berlin,
1883...W. H.

The Blickling Homilies of the Tenth Century:
ed. by R. Morris; E. E. T. S., Nos. 58
and 63. London, 1874 and 1876........B. H.

King Alfred's Anglo-Saxon version of Boethius, *De Consolatione Philosophiae:* ed.
by Rev. Samuel Fox, M. A.; London,
1890. Bohn's Antiq. Liby...............Boeth.

M. S. Boetii: *Philosophiae Consolationis Libri quinque.* Recensuit Rudolfus Peiper; Leipsiae, 1871.

CLASSIFICATION.

Gerber [1] gives the following divisions of Tropes and Figures :—

(1) Picture-figures (*Bildfiguren*), or æsthetic figures, usually called Tropes ;

(2) Phonetic or Sound-figures ;

(3) Figures of thought or sense (*noetische oder Sinn Figuren*). This treatise will deal mainly with the two first divisions, and will include only certain leading figures in these divisions.

The distinction between a trope and a figure has been repeatedly pointed out. Professor H. E. Greene [2] thus renders the definitions of Quintilian, which bring out the distinction as well as anything since written : "A trope is the turning of a word or phrase from its literal signification to another; while 'a figure, as is indicated by its very name,—*figura*,—is a form of speech differing from the common and ordinary mode of expression.' [3] A trope gives a word a new meaning; while a figure is simply a matter of the order of words."

I. TROPES: 1. METAPHOR.

The *Century Dictionary* defines Metaphor as "a figure of speech from which, by some supposed resemblance or analogy, a name, an attribute, or an action, belonging to or characteristic of one object, is assigned to another to which it is not literally applicable; the figurative transfer of a descriptive or affirmative word or phrase from one thing to another; implied comparison by transfer of terms."

In the following lists of metaphors, no special classification is adopted. It is almost impossible to find a system of grouping which is thoroughly satisfactory, and, rather than adopt one that would lead to confusion, or one that would obscure the literary value of the trope, I have arranged them according to their sequence in the texts, and grouped only those of close resemblance in form and meaning.

[1] II, 11.

[2] *Publications of the Modern Language Association of America*, New Series, vol. I, p. 448.

[3] Quintilian: Inst. Orator., IX, i, 4:—Figura, sicut nomine ipso patet. conformatio quædam a communi et primum se offerente ratione.

A. H.

18. 5, næron hi blinde gesceapene,—referring to spiritual blindness; 34. 7, on ðære ures geleafan gafol mid estfullum mode hine agifan; 36. 7, getacnodon ða halgan lareowas on Godes gelaðunge, ðe sind gastlice hyrdas geleaffulra sawla; 36. 14, ðam lareowe gedafenað ðæt he symle wacol sy ofer Godes eowode, ðæt se ungesawenlica wulf Godes sceop ne tostence,—these two metaphors are manifestly suggested by *John* x, 1–18. 36. 28, Christ is se soða dæg, seðe todræfde mid his tocyme ealle nytennysse ðære ealdan nihte and ealne middangeard mid his gife onlihte, so 144. 7,— suggested by *John* viii, 12. 48. 27, on ðam gastlicum gefeohte his martyrdomes,—a common clerical trope. 50. 5, seðe wæs leorning-cniht on hade, ongann wesan lareow on martyrdome; 50. 12, he hæfð ðone ecan wuldorbeah; 52. 12, seo soðe lufu is wylspring and ordfruma ealra godnyssa . . . and se weg ðe læt to heofonum,—notice here the coupling of a figurative and a literal word in 'wylspring' and 'ordfruma' and the change of trope in 'weg.' 52. 14, seðe færð on soðre lufe ne mæg he dwelian; 52. 15, heo [love] gewissað and gescylt and gelæt; 56. 7, ðu bist Godes bearn; 56. 30, Stephen fram lichamlicere wununge gewitende . . . sigefæst to heofenum ferde,—cf. ii. *Cor.* v, 1. 60. 34, ydel bið se læcedom ðe ne mæg ðone untruman gehælan; swa bið eac ydel seo lar ðe ne gehælð ðære sawle leahtras and unðeawas; 62. 4, he syððan hæfde his goldhord on heofenum,—cf. *Matth.* vi, 20. 62. 14, ða wurdon hi mid deofles flan ðurhscotene; 64. 15, beoð blowende and welige hwilwendlice ðæt ge ecelice wædlion; 64. 18, ðæt he do his ðeowan . . . unwiðmetenlice scinan; 66. 6, ne bið he ðæra æhta hlaford, ðonne he hi dælan ne mæg; ac he bið ðæra æhta ðeowa, ðonne he him eallunga ðeowað, so 122. 7; 68. 11, he eowre saula ðe nu synd adylegode of ðære liflican bec, gelædc eft to Godes gife and miltsunge; 70. 7, ðæra gedwolmanna dyrstignesse adwæscte; 72. 23, he mid rodetacne his muðe and ealne his lichaman gewæpenode; 74. 15, tima is ðæt ðu mid ðinum gebroðrum wistfullige on minum gebeorscipe, so 74. 27; 76. 3, geopena ongean nu lifes geat ðær ðæra ðeostra ealdras me ne gemeton; 84. 5, næron hi geripode to slege, ac hi . . . swulton to life; 84. 13, hi sind gehatene martyra blostman, forðan ðe hi wæron swa swa upaspringende blostman on middeweardan cyle ungeleaffulnysse, swilce mid

sumere chtnysse forste forsodene,—the metaphor becomes a simile.
94. 31, buton he ða ymbsnidennysse on gastlicum ðeawum gehealde,
so 96. 8, 26, 33.

110. 32, ydele leasunge adwæscan mid deopnysse godcundra
gewrita; 116. 14, hi offrodon Criste gastlice recels and noldon him
gold offrian, so 116. 17, 20, 142. 12; 118. 5, gif we on his gesihðe
mid beorhtnysse ðæs uplican wisdomes scinende beoð; 118. 7, gif
we ure geðohtas . . . on weofoðe ure heortan onælað, ðæt we
magon . . . wynsumlice . . . stincan, so 118. 16, 18; 118. 28, us
is micel neod þæt we ðurh oðerne weg ðone swicolan deofol forbu-
gan ðæt we moton gesæliglice to urum eðele becuman; 122. 17,
eal mancyn ðe wæs atelic hreoflig, mid mislicum leahtrum on ðam
inran menn, so 122. 23, 124. 11; 122. 25, ðæt he ure saule fram
synna fagnyssum gehælan mæge; 124. 14, his sawle wunda dæd-
betende gelacniau, so 142. 33; 124. 0, ðe swa hreoflic bið on
manfullum ðeawum ðæt he oðre mid his yfelnysse besmit, so 124.
33;—these metaphors, relating to spiritual sickness, are common
in the religious literature. 132. 7, ðe heora heortan wyrtruman on
ðisum . . . life plantiað; 132. 11, ða inran ðeostru sind ðæs modes
blindnyssa wiðinnan, so 132. 12; 138. 22, ðonne on urum mode
bið acenned sum ðing Godes,—this with many other metaphors
has become almost colourless. 138. 28, ure unclænan geðohtas and
weorc, ða we sceolan symle acwellan oððe behwyrfan mid clænum;
146. 16, ne . . . Cristes swurd sceolde ðurhgan Marian lichaman,
ac hyra sawla. Cristes swurd is her gesett, swa swa we cwædon,
for his ðrowunge; 154. 9, we ne magon on ðissum life ðæs ecan
leohtes brucan; 154. 10, ðes an blinda getacnode call mancynn, ðe
wearð ablend ðurh Adames gylt, so 154. 19, 156. 1, 3, 5, 7;—
in these and similar instances, which abound in Ælfric, the metaphor loses nearly all its rhetorical value by the elaborate allegorical
interpretation. 154. 21, abrodene of urum gedwyldum and onlihte
ðurh geleafan; 154. 22, nu hæbbe we ðæt leoht on urum mode,
ðæt is Cristes geleafa; 154. 24, ðeah ðe we gyt lichamlice on urum
cweorterne wunian; 154. 34, ða wearð mancyn onliht and gesihðe
underfeng; 156. 16, ðonne cumað ða ealdan leahtras . . . and hi
gedrefað his mod, and willað gestillan his stemne; 156. 23, ðæt
he todræfe ða yfelan costnunga fram ure heortan and ðæt he
onlihte ure mod mid his gife; 156. 26, ðonne mage we gedon . . .
ðæt se Hælend stent, seðe ær eode; 158. 8, ures modes blindnysse;

158. 17, biŏ ure heorte onbryred and gewend to Gode,—weakened metaphor. 158. 29, biddan ŏæs leohtes ŏe we magon mid englum anum gescon, ŏæt ŏe næfre ne biŏ geendod. To ŏam leohte soŏlice ure geleafa us sceal gebringan,—in the latter half of this quotation we have a weak form of personification. 160. 15, heo [soul] biŏ dead ælcere duguŏe and gesælŏe, and biŏ gehealdan to ŏam ecan deaŏe; 162. 16, nis ŏeos woruld na ure eŏel ac is ure wræcsiŏ,—a forcible metaphor, since exile was the greatest abhorrence of the Anglo-Saxon. 168. 7, Deofol is calra unrihtwisra manna heafod and ŏa yfelan men sind his lima, so 168. 8, 238. 26, 272. 28, 390. 12, 604. 35; 170. 17, Gif we nealæcaŏ urum Drihtne mid geleafan . . .; gif we hwær aslidon, arisan eft ŏærrihte, and betan georne ŏæt ŏær tobrocen biŏ; 170. 23, seŏe gebigde ŏone halgan heofenlican bigels,—one of the few poetic metaphors in prose. 176. 1, ŏonne biŏ oft ŏæs mannes mod gebiged to ŏære lust-fullunge, hwilon eac aslit to ŏære geŏafunge; 184. 10, ŏam he forgifŏ ŏone gastlican fodan ŏæt hi ne ateorian be wege; 188. 7, ŏonne we cumaŏ to ŏam smedman, ŏæt is to ŏære getacnunge, ŏonne gereordaŏ heo [the old law] ure mod; 188. 25, nu sceal gehwa . . . of tredan ŏæt gærs and of sittan, ŏæt is ŏæt he sceal ŏa flæsclican lustas gewyldan,—notice the favourite allegorical interpretation. 188. 29, ŏa menn ŏe to ŏam gastlican gereorde belimpaŏ, so 190. 2; 198. 35, heo wæs geclænsod and gescyld wiŏ ealle leahtras.

204. 8, gif we mid ŏam gewitendlicum gestreonum beceapaŏ him ŏæt ece lif and ŏa heofonlican welan mid Gode; 208. 2, hi wæron getigede, forŏon ŏe eal mancyn wæs mid synnum bebunden, so 208. 5, 20, 22, 23; 210. 35, we beoŏ tempel and fætels ŏæs Halgan Gastes, so 210. 4, 262. 16, 17,—a Biblical metaphor; cf. 1 *Corinth.* vi. 19. 212. 10, hi ne magon his geoc of heora swuran asceacan; 212. 13, gif he mid deofles weorcum hine sylfne bebint, ŏonne ne mæg he mid his anre mihte hine unbindan butan . . . God . . . hine unbindan, so 234. 14; 216. 15, gefredde ŏa ŏone engel Cristes godcundnysse, ŏurh ŏa he wæs to deaŏe aceocod, so 216. 31; 218. 23, se lichama, ŏe is ŏære sawle reaf; 222. 3, gif we beoŏ gefyllede mid bræŏe haligra mihta, and gif we mid hlysan godra weorca urne Drihten secaŏ; 222. 6, ŏa gesceoŏ ŏa heofonlican Englas ŏa ŏe mid bræŏum godra weorca gewilniaŏ ŏæs upplican færeldes; 226. 2, nu sind adwæscede ealle geleaflystu; 226. 15, he ŏone deaŏ

mid his æriste tobræc; 226. 19, his nama adwæsced; 228. 1, ure
Hælend Crist tobræc helle-gatu; 234. 9, ða unbindan fram heora
synnum ða ðe Crist geliffæst; 238. 29, ælc bisceop and ælc lareow
is to hyrde gesett Godes folce, so 560. 34; 240. 1, se wulf is deofol,
ðe syrwð ymbe Godes gelaðunge and cepð hu he mæge cristenra
manna sawla mid leahtrum fordon; 248. 14, we ealle sind cuman
on ðisum life, and ure eard nis na her; ac we sind her swilce wegferende menn; 248. 25, clypigan to Criste and biddan ðæra ðreora
hlafa; 250. 1, nu sceole we cnucian, and hryman to Criste; 252. 16,
ðonne bið ure hiht gehealden wið ðæs wyrmes slege; 254. 28, se
rica and se ðearfa sind wegferende on ðisre worulde. Nu berð se
rica swære byrðene his gestreona and se ðearfa færð æmtig; 254. 34,
ealle we sind Godes ðearfan; 256. 17, seo gytsung is ealra yfelra
wyrtruma; 256. 18, ðe fyligað ðære gytsunge, hi dweliað fram
Godes geleafan, and hi befeallað on mislice costnunga and deri-
gendlice lustas, ðe hi besencað on forwyrd; 264. 27, gehealde and
gescylde ge ure sawle ge urum lichaman, fram deofles costnungum;
264. 34, and sylle eac ure sawle ðone gastlican hlaf. Se gastlica
hlaf is Godes bebod; 266. 11, mid ðam gastlican gereorde ure sawle
geclænsian and getrymman; 286. 17, ðære heofenan frætwunge;
288. 7, Godes Gast afandað ealra manna heortan and ða ðe on hine
gelyfað . . . ða he clænsað and geglaðað mid his neosunge,—note
the combination of literal and metaphorical statement. 298. 4, ða
com se Halga Gast on fyres hiwe to ðam halgum hyrede . . . and
he ealle onælde mid undergendlicum fyre and hi wæron afyllede
mid ðære heofonlican lare.

320. 20, hi wæron byrnende on Godes willan, so 344. 7, 10,
346. 23; 320. 23, ðære hæðenra manna heortan ðe cealde wæron
ðurh geleaflæste . . . gewilnunga; 322. 7, ðæt hi [men's hearts]
beoð liðe ðurh unscæððignysse, and onælede ðurh lufe and snoternysse, so 322. 13, 14, 324. 6; 332. 31, ne lufað se hine sylfne
seðe hine mid synnum bebint; 338. 20, mid hete ðæt tældon; 360.
11, campian dæghwamlice wið leahtras, and hine sylfne ðreagian
mid styrnysse ðære gastlican steore; 360. 21, unlustas mid agenre
cynegyrde gestyran; 362. 27, ðe beoð ðurh unrihtwisnysse hocas
awegde, eft ðurh regolsticcan ðære soðan rihtwisnysse beoð geem-
node; 362. 29, scearpnyssa beoð awende to smeðum wegum, ðonne
ða yrsigendan mod . . . gecyrrað to manðwærnysse ðurh ongyte
ðære upplican gife; 374. 22, mid gastlicum gecampe winnað

ongean ðone dry ; 382. 17, ðæt ic sceolde mid ðysre ðrowunge
his fotswaðum fylian . . .; ne gelette ge minne weg, so 382. 19 ;
390. 23, ðæt bilewite scep ða gefullode ðone arleasan Saulum and
worhte hine arfæstne Paulum.   He gefullode ðone wulf and
geworhte to lambe,—note the curious mixture of literal and metaphorical terms.   The metaphor is suggested by the meaning of
Ananias, which Ælfric says is "sheep."

410. 24, ðonne bið eal seo getimbrung hire smeagung toworpen ;
412. 22, gastlice ofsleað mid heora yfelnysse heora underðeoddan ;
414. 5, he wæs toðunden on modignysse, and his flæsclicum lustum
underðeod, and mid ungefohre gytsunge ontend,—notice three
metaphors in immediate succession.   428. 30, næfð min niht nane
forsworcennysse, ac heo mid beorhtum leohte scinð, so 446. 2 ;
472. 12, God is soða læce, ðe ðurh mislice swingla his folces synna
gehælð, so II 560. 33 ; 492. 14, se mann se tosæwð ungeðwærnysse
betwux cristenum mannum ; 492. 15, ðurh his muðes geat, so
492. 16 ; 474. 26, ne beceapige na . . . mid his sawle ðæs lichaman
gesundfulnysse ; 492. 19, macað hi his eare him sylfum to deaðes
geate ; 496. 12, on deaðe geswetod, so II 260. 18 ; 496. 14, heo
[soul] ðurh synna dead is, so 496. 13, II 260. 18 ; 496. 31, ðeah ðe
heo on gewunelicum synnum fule stince ; 496. 33, swa mare wund
swa heo maran læcedomes behofað ; 498. 5, swa bið eac se digla
deað ðære sawle eaðelicor to aræronne . . . ðonne synd ða openan
leahtras to gehælenne.

516. 7, seo hand getacnað urne nydbehefan freond . . .; ac ðeah
gif swilc freond us fram Godes wege gewemð, ðonne bið us selre
ðæt we his flæsclican lufe fram us accorfan, and mid twæminge
awurpon, ðonne we, ðurh his yfelan tihtinge, samod mid him
on ece forwyrd befeallon,—mixture of metaphorical and literal
expression.   520. 27, se halige gelaðung is Cristes bryd, ðurh
ða he gestrynð . . . gastlice bearn, so II 10. 29, II 54. 14, 17,
II 58. 23, II 72. 28, II 476. 31 ; 522. 25, fynd mid horne lichamlicere mihte potedon ; 522. 27, ða sind gemæste mid gife ðæs
Halgan Gastes to ðam swiðe, ðæt hi wilniað ðæs upplican færeldes
mid fyðerum gastlicum drohtnunge ; 522. 31, seðe mid fodan ðære
upplican lufe bið gefylled ; 524. 13, ðæs ecan lifes welan,—a
colourless metaphor.   526. 28, se clæne hwæte bið gebroht on
Godes berne ; ðæt is, ðæt ða rihtwisan beoð gebrohte to ðam ecan
life, ðær ne cymð storm ne nan unweder ðæt ðam corne derie ;

528. 24, ðe mid horium reafe cymð to Godes gyftum, ðæt he for his fulum gyrelan fram ðære ecan blisse ascofen beo into ecum ðeostrum; 542. 35, sind gewuldorbeagode mid sige heora ðrowunga on ecere myrhðe; 544. 18, Godes lare . . . to unateorigendlicum gafele; 552. 17, ne bið God gesewen buton mid clænre heortan; 560. 34, efne her is ure hyrde, efne her is se frefrigend ures geswinces; 578. 25, mid manegum swingelum . . . geswencte, so 578. 26; 578. 28, to lifes wege fylian; 578. 32, underðeodde ðeoda swuran his geoce; 584. 30, mid heora mode heofonum genealæcan; 594. 27, ne onæl ðu ðe sylfum ðæt ece fyr; 602. 17, gefyrn scean leoht ingehydes geond eorðan ymbhwyrft, and forwel menige scinað on soðfæstnysse wege, ða ðe farað ðurh godspellic siðfæt to ðæs ecan lifes gefean; 602. 35, he toscoc ða dwollican nytennysse ðurh onlihtinge his andwerdnysse, swa swa se beorhta dæg todræfð ða dimlican ðeostra ðære sweartan nihte,—notice the simile as an elaboration of the metaphor.   612. 29, heora heortan wyrtruman on his lufe aplantodon; 614. 8, ðæt ðises middangeardes wæstm is hryre. To ðam he wext ðæt he fealle; to ðy he sprytt ðæt he mid ewyldum fornyme swa hwæt swa he ær sprytt; 614. 29, gewitað ða genipu ure dreorignysse; 616. 23, swa hwa swa ungeclænsod bið, he gefret ðæs fyres cðm.

A. H. II.

8. 20, swaðeah ðone liflican wæstm abær, seðe is soð Bisceop and ure sawla alysend; 10. 31, seo gelaðung is ealra cristenra manna moder on gastlicere acennednysse; 14. 29, nu is he gesmyrod . . . mid scofonfealdre gife ðæs Halgan Gastes; 58. 11, ðas six wæter-fatu wæron afyllede mid halwendum wætere boclicra gewrita; 68. 16, ðas sind gemengde ða godan ceastergewaran and ða yfelan swa swa corn and ceaf, oððæt se Dema cymð, ðe gegaderað ðæt clæne corn into his berne, ðæt sind, ða rihtwisan into heofonan rice,—note the combination of the simile and the allegorical interpretation of the metaphor.   70. 10, he sparode ðæt god win oð his agenum tocyme, ðæt he sceneð nu geond his gelaðunge oð ende ðyses middaneardes; 74. 16, buton ða lareowas sereadian symle ða leahtras ðurh heora lare aweg, ne bið ðæt læwede folc wæstmbære on godum weoreum; 76. 2, hi forgyme-leasodon ðæs ecan lifes teolunge; 78. 6, he ne teolað nanes

wæstmes ðæs godcundlican weorces; 78. 35, seðe neorxena wanges
fæsten mid his agenum deaðe geopenode; 88. 26, hi ne adræfað ure
sawla hafenleaste; 88. 28, rihtwisnysse speda and ðæs heofenlican
wisdomes goldhordas; 92. 11, ðæs modes ðrotan,—an example of
Catachresis. 98. 11, swa ageaf ðes goda mann his wæstm Gode.

106. 5, seo ælmysse ure synna lig adwæscte; 124. 6, geope-
nige ure sarnys us infær soðre gecyrrednysse and ðæt wite ðe
we ðrowiað tobrece ure heortan heardnysse; 124. 9, mid swurde
ðæs heofonlican graman, so II 126. 1; 126. 30, Gode wæstmbære
wurde; 132. 24, Cuthberhtus . . . scinende on manegum gecar-
mungum; 136. 28, ðry heofonlice hlafas, on lilian beorhtnysse
scinende and on hrosan bræðe stymende,—cf. B. H. 7. 29. 156. 31,
ðurh ðære hyde wunda adwæscte his modes wunda; 160. 25,
blindnysse his heortan; 180. 31, his wælhreowan hneccan to ðæs
halgan weres fotswaðum gebigde; 188. 13, ðæt scræf . . . on
wundrum scinende; 210. 35, we buton yfelnysse beorman on
ðeorfnysse syfernysse and soðfæstnysse; 236. 20, hi hæfdon stænene
heardnysse on heora heortan; 242. 31, heora andgit aðwoh fram
eallum horwum healicra leahtra; 248. 26, ða spætlu aðwogen ure
sweartan gyltas; 266. 13, we beoð gemearcode ægðer ge on foran
heafde ge on heortan mid blode ðære drihtenlican ðrowunge;
278. 24, we sceoldan wistfullian na on yfelnysse beorman ac on
ðeorfnyssum syfernysse and soðfæstnysse; 288. 32, on geswinc-
fullum yðum ðises deadlican lifes, so II 290. 3, 33, II 388. 6,
7,—metaphors from the sea are rare in prose, but abundant in
poetry.

294. 10, mid leohte ures geleafan; 318. 27, fiðera ðære soðan lufe;
320. 22, buton he ærest arise of ðam reocendum meoxe and mid
soðre dædbote him sylfne aðwea; 374. 8, to ðam estum ðæs ecan
gereordes; 374. 30, ðæt leoht ðæs larlican andgites; 388. 9, windige
ehtnysse astyrige ongean Cristes gelaðunge; 388. 16, geendodre
nihte unrihtwisnysse; 392. 22, on ðissere worulde hreohnyssum;
392. 26, gif ðu lufast ðas woruld, heo besencð ðe; 392. 28, gif
ðin heorte floterað on ðissere worulde gytsunge; 392. 32, hawa
ðæt se inra wind ðe ne towende; 392. 35, gif ðu hwilon dyfst
ðurh woruldlicum lustfullungum; 398. 5, to ðam wynsuman geoce
Godes ðeowdomes; 398. 10, mete ðære halgan lare; 402. 11, heora
heortan wyrtruman on ðam liflican wylle; 404. 14, hiwiað hi

wiðutan mid cawfæstum ðeawum, and wiðinnan sind geættrode mid
arleasnysse; 408. 26, uton beon wæstmbære on godum weorcum, ði
læs ðe se Hælend us wæstmlease gemete, and hate us mid deaðes
eaxe forceorfan ; 470. 16, ðam heofonlicum læcedome; 478. 12,
mid wuldorbeage eces mægðhades, so II 494. 32 ; 512. 34, sccan
on witegunge; 526. 15, wæstm godra dæda ; 526. 18, ðara apos-
tola wæstm ; 532. 31, ne his agene weorc mid deadum fellum
ymbtrymman ; 534. 2, hwæt doð ðas buton swilce hi heora fet
mid deadra nytena fellum beteon?—the conclusion of an allegorical
interpretation.   538. 23, hi [evils] sind ða hydelas ðæs ccan lifes,
ðe yfelum mannum becymð for heora anwillan yfelnysse; 546. 2,
Godes gelaðung hæfð on sibbe lilian, ðæt is clæne drohtnung; on
ðam gewinne, rosan, ðæt is, martyrdom ; 554. 19, God of gæð his
feoh æt eow mid ðam gastlican gafole ; 556. 32, his unlustes
ðeostra ; 560. 28, fela blindra manna, ðe fram soðfæstnysse wege
dwelodon, he onlihte ðurh ða soðan lare, so II 560. 28 ; 602. 4,
seo soðe behreowsung and dædbot . . . us aðwehð eft fram ðam
synnum ; 602. 12, dædbot . . . and ælmesdæda . . . gehælað and
gelacniað ure synna, gif we ða læcedomas geornlice begað.

W. H.

1. 9, ðrem modes leohte ; 3. 14, ðe we nu on carcerne syn bety-
nede on ðisse worulde, and eft ðonne se gast wyrð ut of ðam
lichoman alæd ðe he nu mid befangen is ; 18. 1, gerymed hæfð us
callum rihtne weg ; 35. 17, ðæt deofol ne mæg ænig his ættrenra
wæpna him on afæstnjan ; he bið ðonne Cristes lima an, so 37. 6,
65. 19, 79. 1, 310. 15 ; 40. 3, beorgað eow georne wið deofles lara,
so 40. 8, 11, 21 ; 67. 14, ane gastlice modor, seo is ecclesia gena-
mod,—a universal metaphor.   71. 15, sona wyrð heofona rices
duru geara untyned ; 75. 22, ure lifwegas geornlice rihtan ; 79. 13,
nu is mycel neod eac eallum Godes bydelum, ðæt hy Godes fole
warnjan gelome wið ðone egesan ðe mannum is toweard ; 80. 1, we
godcunde heorda warnjan nu georne ; 103. 29, gebohte [mankind]
deorwyrðan ceape ; 139. 13, flyhð se frofur aweg ; 156. 4, ðeos
woruld is on ofste and hit nealæcð ðam ende ; 156. 10, unrihta to
fela ricsode on lande ; 158. 8, Godes hus syndon to clæne berypte
ealdra gerihta and innan bestrypte ælcra gerysena, so 157. 18 ;

178. 8, swær is seo byrðen, ðe Godes bydel beran mot; 178. 22,
ðam godcundan hyrdan; 180. 15, forðam ðe hit [absolution] is
ealra læcedoma selost; 180. 8, clænsige his heortan gehwa fram
æghwilcum niðgraman; 186. 13, se fyrena ren; 190. 16, wa ðam
hirdum . . . ðe estað heom silfum . . . and godcundre heorde ne
gimeð to nahte, so 191. 7, 12, 16; 228. 13, ðonne beoð eow opene
heofena geatu; 230. 19, rinan mannum ðone heofonlican mete;
232. 23, cyrice is ðære sawle scip and scild on domes dæg, and heo
is us gesceapen to gebedhuse, na to nanum gemothuse; 236. 15,
ðære fyrenan ea; 239. 7, heo [the Church] bið ure friðjend and
werigend wið ðæt micele fyr on domes dæg; 239. 13, eac beðearf
seo sawul on domes dæg rihtes weges and clænes and staðolfæstre
brycge ofer ðone glideran weg hellewites brogan; 239. 15, bærnon
we urne lichaman mid clænum gebedum æt urum heortan; 242. 3,
oferfyll bið ðære sawle feond and ðæs lichaman unhæl; 242. 9,
hit alueð ðæs mannes mod ðurh deofles costnunge; 243. 19, ær
man aweodige ða unriht and ða manweorc, ðe man wide sæwð
and gesawen hæfð; 247. 6, he sceal beon grundweall ðines lifes,
and se liht sceal beon ðin scyld ealles ðines lifes; 247. 8, seo soðe
lufu sceal beon ðin wundorbeah; 247. 13, ðæt sint feower sweras
. . . iustitia, etc.; 249. 2, se modiga deofol . . . wyle wið ðinre
sawle campjan; 251. 15, we wæron gefriðode feonda gafoles;
252. 1, stænenre heortan and blindre; 252. 4, ðone unrihtan
wrigels of heora heortan and heo onbyrhte mid leohtum andgite;
252. 8, he him mildheortnesse earan ontynde; 252. 10, ærðam we
wæron steopcild gewordene, forðam ðe we wæron astypede ðæs
heofenlican rices; 252. 17, se facna feond ne us ne forwyrne ðæs
wilweges ne us ða gata ne betyne . . . ne us ðære byrig ne ofteo;
257. 21, ðone weallendan welm; 273. 8, heo is ðeos woruld on
ofstum and on stormum and on adlum and on ungewyderum;
276. 4, ða hyrdas, ðe na cunnan ða godcundan heorde healdan,
so 276. 11; 302. 29, cyrice bið ure scyld and nerjend on domes
dæg wið ðæt micele fyr.

B. H.

3. 11, se Halga Gast seow ðæt clæne sæd on ðone unbesmitenan
innoð; 5. 19, innoð . . . ðæt wæs ðæt templ ðære geðungennesse
and ealre clænnesse; 7. 25, sy ðæt geteld aðened ðines innoðes;

7. 26, seo onblawnes ðære heofonlican onfæðmnesse sy gewindwod on ðe; 7. 28, sy ðin ðæt fæðmlice hrif mid callum fægernessum gefrætwod; 7. 29, seo readnes ðære rosan lixeð on ðe and seo hwitnes ðære lilian scineð on ðe; 7. 31, mid callum missenlicum afeddum blostmum sy se Cristes brydbur gefrætwod; 7. 33, to hwon yldestu middangeard to onlyhtenne; 7. 35, ðæs Hehstan mægen ðe ymbscineð; 9. 4, God ðe hafað to gisle her on middangearde geseted; 9. 9, se heofonlica Cyning gearwað ðinne innoð his Suna to brydbure and on ðam brydlocan micelne gefean; 9. 26, Drihten on ðære fæmnan brydbure and on ðæm gerisnlican hehsetle onfeng lichoman gegyrelan to his godcundnesse; 9. 28, he wæs gesended ðæt goldhord ðæs mægen-ðrymmes on ðone bend ðæs clænan innoðes; 9. 35, he becom to ðæm heahsetle ðære rode on ðæm upstige eall ure lif he getremede; 9. 36, he scalde his ðone readan gim, ðæt wæs his ðæt halige blod; 11. 5, gifeon . . . on ðone gemanan ðæs brydguman and ðære bryde, ðæt is Crist and seo halige cyrice, so 11. 30; 11. 28, astag ðæt heofonlice goldhord on ðysne ymbhwyrft fram ðæm heahsetle ure gescyppendes; 11. 34, he us gesohte on ðas ælðeodignesse; 13. 10, ðonne bið Drihten ure se trumesta staðol and se selosta scyld wið eallum deofles costnungum, so 89. 10; 13. 23, ne bið ðær Cristes eardung ne his wunung on ðære heortan; 15. 13, hie wæron him bediglede, forðon ðe hie wæron ðagyt mid worldgeðohtum bewrigene; 17. 33, seðe ne can ða beorhtnesse ðæs ecan leohtes, se bið blind, so 17. 14, 36; 19. 9, seo stemn ðære heortan bið swiðe gedrefed on ðæm gebede; 19. 15, mid mycelum hungre yfelra geðohta abisgode; 19. 24, ðære godcundnesse nænig onwendnesse on carcerne wæs of ðære menniscan gecynde; 19. 28, ure stefne blindnesse gehyreð; 21. 6, his eagena leohtes; 21. 16, oðon leohte is fulfremednesse weg ðe we on feran, so 21. 17, 18; 23. 2, ða blindnesse ure ælðeodignesse; 23. 2, we send on ðisse worulde ælðeodignesse; we synd on ðisse worlde ælðeodige; 25. 6, hie beoð upahafene on oforhygde and eac beoð onbærnde mid ðære biteran refeste, ge eac beoð besmitene mid ðem unclænan firenluste; 27. 23, ðam fulwihtes bræde; 29. 11, ðæm æspringe Godes mildheortnesse; 37. 8, mid ðære swetnesse godcundra beboda, so 55. 21, 23; 37. 18, seðe wille Drihtne bringan geeweme lac fæsten; 41. 12, ne ðurfon ge wenan ðæt ge ðæt orceape sellon, ðæt ge under Drihtnes borh syllað.

45. 25, Cristenra folces hyrdas; 51. 11, ontyneð us Drihten heofenes ðeotan; 53. 14, on ðæm heofonlican goldhorde; 55. 7, se
wyrtruma ðære halgan gesegene of his heortan bið alocen and
onweg anumen; 55. 27, hie gastlice wæstm ne berað . . .; forðon
ðe ðæt halige sæd on him gedwan and gewat, ðæt him ær of ðæs
lareowes muðe wæs bodad and sægd; 57. 11, seo saul gif heo ne
bið mid Godes worde feded gastlice hungre and ðurste heo bið
cwelmed; 59. 5, ðonne se geogoð-had ærest bloweð and fægerost
bið; 63. 10, hi beoð betuh him sylfum slitende wulfas; 65. 3,
ðæt hit sy wyrtruma ealra oðerra synna; 71. 36, wæstm godra
weorca; 73. 29, godra weorca swetne stenc; 75. 9, swa sæt ðonne
seo unaræfnedlice byrðen synna on eallum ðysum menniscan
cynne; 77. 10, he hine ær of sawle deaðe awehte; 83. 21, æfter
ðæm bendum his deaðes, and æfer ðæm clammum helle ðeostra.
89. 16, ic eom dust and axe; 91. 12, he us mid his blode abohte
of helle hæftnede; 95. 2, mycele herehyð manna saula; 97. 30,
ðone læcedom ure sauwle; 105. 14, on ðam gecorenan hordfæte;
105. 26, hie wæron stænenre heortan and blindre; 105. 29, God
afyrde him ðæt unriht wrigels of heora heortan and hie onbyrhte mid
leohtum andgite; 107. 1, he him mildheortnesse earon ontynde,—
cf. W. H., p. 251 ff. 107. 14, to ðam selran and to ðon soðon
læcedome; 109. 3, colað . . . seo lufu; 109. 31, ða synbyrðenna;
115. 7, he [world] wæs blowende . . . on swyðe manigfealdre
wynsumnesse, so 115. 13; 133. 23, hie inneweardum heortan ecelice
burnon ðære Godes lufan; 135. 7, ða myclan byrðenne . . . ðære
myclan langunga; 141. 1, ðu eart lifes swer; 145. 4, we bærnan
gastlico leohtfato; 145. 6, he hie onlyhte mid his ðæs Halgan Gastes
gife; 147. 36, ðinra beboda goldhord; 149. 2, ne forlæte ic ðe næfre,
min meregrot . . . min corelanstan, forðon ðe ðu eart soðlice Godes
templ, so 153. 6, 155. 32; 157. 1, ðu ðe gecure ðæt fæt on to
eardienne; 157. 11, aris ðu, min se nehste and min culufre and mines
wuldres eardung and forðon ðe ðu eart lifes fæt and ðu eart ðæt heo-
fenlice templ; 163. 11, ðære halignesse hus geclænsod beon sceolde,
and seo gastliðnes ðæs Cristes wiesceaweres and seo gifernes gebuend
wæs ðæs Cristes engles and seo heall ðæs Halgan Gastes swylc
templ eallunga Gode weorðe funden; 163. 20, he wæs gelic Godes
englum, and he wæs beme, Cristes fricca on ðysne middangeard
and wæs Godes sunu spellboda and segnbora ðæs ufancundan

kyninges and firena forgifnes and gerihtnes hæðenra ðeoda,—
notice the opening simile with the metaphor immediately following.
163. 30, se niwa eorendel, Sanctus Johannes; 163. 30, se leoma
ðære soðan sunnan, God; 163. 32, seo beme Sanctus Johannes;
165. 1, he mid ðære soðfæstnesse stefne gehiered wæs; 185. 6, he
bi'ð gedyped on ða neoðemestan helle witu; 207. 9, mid haligra
lofsanga lacum; 225. 17, cuma'ð arisende wulfas, todrifa'ð ðine
heorde; 225. 36, seo Godes lufu to ðæs hat and to ðæs beorht on
his heortan; 229. 23, minra eagena leoht; 241. 3, ana ðu heardeste
stræl to æghwilere unrihtnesse; ðu ðe simle fihtest wið manna
cyn; 241. 5, Crist ðe gehnæde in helle.

BOETH.

4. 9, me ablendon ðas ungetreowan woruldsæl'ða, and me forletan
swa blindne on ðisse dimme hol; 4. 21, ðu hæfst ðara wæpna to
hrade forgiten ðe ic ðe ær scalde; 4. 23, gewita'ð nu awirgede
woruldsorga of mines ðegenes Mode, forðam ge sind ða mæstan
sceaðan,—the original has a mythological allusion, which, because
it would be unintelligible to the Anglo-Saxon, is avoided in the
translation—sed abite potius Sirenes usque in exitum dulcis mei-
sque cum musis curandum sanandumque relinquete (I i. 37). 4. 27,
adrigde ða mines Modes eagan; 4. 31, ac hit ongeat his lare swiðe
totorenne and swiðe tobrocenne mid dysigra hondum; 6. 7, Eala
on hu grundleasum sceaðe ðæt Mod ðringð ðonne hit bestyrma'ð
ðisse worulde ungeðwærnessa,—the Latin corresponds—Heu quam
præcipiti mersa profundo Mens hebet et propria luce relicta Tendit
in externas ire tenebras (I ii. 1). 6. 9, gif hit ðonne forget his
agen leoht, ðæt is ece gefea, and ðringð on ða fremdan ðistro, ðæt
sind woruldsorga,—corresponding to the second part of the Latin
just quoted—"et propria luce relicta etc." 8. 15, sticia'ð gehydde
beorhte cræftas,—Latet obscuris condita virtus Clara tenebris (I v.
34), the greater vividness of the Latin will be noticed. 8. 22,
forðam hit nu eall winð on ðam yðum ðisse worulde,—the same
idea occurs in the Latin—Rapidos rector comprime fluctus et quo
coelum regis immensum Firma stabiles fædere terras (I v. 46).
8. 28, ðu wære utafaren of ðines Fæder eðele, ðæt is of minum
larum,—notice the explanation of the figure, and the greater

picturesqueness of the A. S., when compared with the Latin—ilico miserum exsulemque cognovi (i v. 3); the same idea occurs in 8. 32,—ic wiste ðæt ðu utafaren wære, ac ic nyste hu feor etc.— to which corresponds the Latin—sed quam id longinquam esset exilium . . . nesciebam (i v. 4). 12. 31, nu ic habbe ongiten ðine ormodnesse . . . ac ic wat hu ðin man getilian sceal,—the Latin has—Iam scio . . . morbi tui . . . causam; quid ipse sis, nosse desisti, quare plenissime vel ægritudinis tuæ rationem vel aditum reconciliandæ sospitatis inveni (i vi. 36). 12. 33, ðu rædest ðæt ðu wrecca wære and bereafod ælces godes,—the Latin, exsulem te et expoliatum propriis bonis esse doluisti (i vi. 40). 14. 9, we habbað nu geot ðone to mæstan dæl ðære tyndran ðinre hæle,— the Latin is the same,—habemus maximum tuæ fomitem salutis veram de mundi gubernatione sententiam (i vi. 48). 14. 12, forðam ðe of ðam lytlan spearcan ðe ðu mid ðære tyndran gefenge lifes leoht ðé onlihte,—jam tibi ex hac minima scintillula vitalis color inluxerit (i vi. 51). 14. 17, of ðæm ðonne onginnað weaxan ða mistas ðe ðæt Mod gedrefað and mid ealle fordwilmað ða soðan gesichðe swelce mistas swelce nu on ðinum Mode sindan—ex quibus orta purturbationum caligo verum illum confundit intuitum (i vi. 55). 14. 19, ac ic hie sceal ærest gedinnian, ðæt ic siððan ðy eð mæge ðæt soðe leoht on ðe gebringan,—to which corresponds—hanc paulisper lenibus mediocribusque fomentis attenuare temptabo, ut dimotis fallacium affectionum tenebris splendorem veræ lucis possis agnoscere (i vi. 56). The original is more affective than the translation.

14. 30, swa doð nu ða ðeostro ðinre gedrefednesse wiðstandan minum leohtum larum,—suggested by the Latin—Nubibus atris condita nullum Fundere possunt Sidera lumen (i vii. 1). 14. 31, ac gif ðu wilnige on rihtum geleafan ðæt soðe leoht oncnawan, etc. The Latin contains the same trope—Tu quoque si vis Lumine claro Cernere verum, etc. (i vii. 20). 16. 1, ðæt Mod siemle bið gebunden mid gedrefednesse ðær ðissa twega yfela anðer ricsað,—so in the Latin—Nubila mens est Vinctaque frenis, Hæc ubi regnant (i vii. 29). 16. 9, ic ongite genoh sweotule ðæt ða woruld sælða mid swiðe manigre swetnesse swiðe lytelice oleccað ðæm Modum ðe hi on last willað swiðost beswican,—this may also be con- sidered as an example of Personification; the Latin is—Intelligo

2

multiformes illius prodigii fucos et eo usque cum his quos eludere nititur blandissimam familiaritatem, dum intolerabili dolore confundat quos insperata reliquerit (II i. 6). 18. 2, nu ðu hæfst ongiten ða wonclan trnwa ðæs blindan lustes,—the Latin has a more vivid trope—deprehendisti Cæci numinis ambiguos vultus (II i. 31). 18. 6, gif ðu ðonne heora ðegen [i. e. of worldly goods] beon wilt; so 20. 33, mine ðeowas sindon Wisdomas and Cræftas and soðe welan. 22. 31, ne hið se ðurst gefylled heora gitsunga ac seo grundlease swelgend hæfð swiðe manegu westu holu on to gadrianne,—Sed quæsita vorans sæva rapacitas Alios pandit hiatus (II ii. 13). 30. 5, ðin ancor is git on corðan fæst,—quando tenaces hærent ancoræ (II iv. 29); so 30. 10, eala wæran ða ancras swa trume and swa ðurhwuniende ge for Gode ge for worulde,—the Latin is—et hærcatet inquam precor (II iv. 31); so 30. 13, call hie us ðyncað ðy leohtran ða hwile ðe ða ancras fæste beoð.

32. 34, mid swiðe mænige biternesse is gemenged seo swetnes ðisse worulde, so the original—Quam multis amaritudinibus humanæ felicitatis dulcedo respersa est (II iv. 61). 32. 35, ðeah heo hwam wynsum ðynce, ne mæg he hie ne habban gif heo hine fleon onginð,—the original is less vivid in the use of 'abeat' which the A. S. translator renders by the more concrete 'fleon'—tamen quominus cum velit abeat, retinere non possit (II iv. 63). 34. 2, ne hie [wealth] ðam geðyldegum . . . simble ne wuniað,—the metaphor is not the same in the Latin, but the personification exists in both—nec apud æquanimos perpetua pendurat nec anxios tota delectat (II iv. 66). 34. 7, se hrof is callra gesælða,—to which the Latin corresponds, but with a different metaphor—summa cardinem felicitatis (II iv. 69). Further instances of this metaphor, with the Latin correspondent, are as follows: 60. 22, beoð to ðam hrofe ðonne git cumen fulfremedra mægena,—ad extreman manum virtutum perfectione perductas (II vii. 6),—the different metaphor is to be noticed. 80. 13, ðæt is hrof callra oðerra goda; the Latin is not metaphorical—omnium summum bonorum (III ii. 7). 80. 19, hit is ægðer ge hrof ge flor ealles godes,—not a direct translation of the Latin,—bonorum omnium congregatione (III ii. 11)—but suggested, apart from the peculiar A. S. trope, by the meaning. 136. 10, he is fruma and æwelm and hrof callra goda,—the metaphor is not in the Latin, the corresponding language being quite

literal. 142. 30, ðæt hehste god is hrof callra oðra goda, so
142. 34, ðæt hehste god sie ðe (se) hehsta hrof callra goda and seo
hior ðe eall god on hwearfað,—the Latin has only the metaphor of
the 'hinge'—Quo fit, uti summa, cardo atque causa expetendorum
omnium bonitas esse jure credatur (III x. 121). 154. 8, he sie se
hehsta hrof callra Goda,—to which—erit omnium summum bonorum (III x. 110). 180. 12, irnað hider and ðider dwoligende
under ðam hrofe callra gesceafta,—the Latin here is closer to the
A. S. than any previous example under this head—circa ipsam
rerum summam virticemque deficiunt (IV ii. 78). 180. 17, to
ðam hehstan hrofe callra gesceafta ðæt is God ; 184. 13, he is ælces
godes ægðer ge hrof ge flor; 224. 26, to ðæm hean hrofe callra
goda,—note the different metaphor in the Latin—de summi boni
cardine (IV vi. 95). 226. 22, he of ðæm hean hrofe hit eall
gesihð,—which is very close to the Latin—qui cum ex alta pro-
videntiæ specula respexit (IV vi. 115). 254. 16, wið ðæs hean
hrofes ðæs hehstan andgites,—corresponding to the Latin—in illius ·
summæ intellegentiæ cacumen (V v. 49),—the translation in this
case is more exact.

36. 18, ðonne hit se wind strongra geswinca astyroð, oððe se
ren ungemetlices ymbhogan; 36. 20, he sceal fleon ðone frecnan
wlite ðises middangeardes and timbrian ðæt hus Modes on ðam
fæstan stane caðmetta,—to which—Fugiens periculosam Sortem
sedis amœnæ Humili domum memento Certus figere saxo (II iv.
13); 36. 22, Crist cardað on ðære dene eadmodnesse,—the idea
was probably suggested by the Latin—Tu conditus quieti Felix
robore valli (II iv. 19). 36. 28, ðeah ðe se wind ðara carfoða
and seo singale gemen ðissa woruldselða him onblawe,—this is
suggested by the Latin—Quamvis tonet ruinis Miscens æquora
ventus, . . . Duces serenus ævum Ridens ætheris iras (II iv. 21),
but fails to be as vivid and effective as the original. In the
'metre' from which these four examples are taken, it is to be
noted that the language of the Latin is not metaphorical.

38. 21, his heortan diegelnesse hit geopenað and ðæs oðres heortan
belocene hit ðurhfærð ; 54. 20, him gedafiað ðæt hi bioð heora
[wealth] hlafordas; 56. 18, ac hine gebindað ða won wilnunga
mid heora unabindendlicum racentum,—corresponding exactly to
the Latin—quem vitiosæ libidines insolubilibus adstrictum retinent

catenis (ɪɪ v. 56). 68. 15, of ðam carcerne ðæs lichoman,—to which—mens conscia terreno carcere soluta. 68. 26, hwi ge wilnigen ðæt ge underlutan mid cowrum swiran ðæt deaðlicne geoc,—to which—colla mortali jugo Frustra levare gestiunt (ɪɪ vii. 7). 70. 18, se æfterra deað gegripð and on eenesse gehæft,—Cum sera vobis rapiet hoc etiam dies, Iam vos secunda mors manet (ɪɪ vii. 25). 74. 5, se anwealda hæfð ealle his gesceafta swa mid his bridle befangene and getogene and gemanode swa ðæt hi nauðer ne gestillan ne moton, ne eac swiðor styrian ðonne he him ðæt gerum his wealdleðeres toforlæt,—this metaphor is contained later on in the Latin, and is translated thus—74. 31, ac ðonne ær ðe he ðæt gewealdleðer forlæt ðara bridla, ðe he ða gesceafta nu mid gebridlode hæfð, &c.; the original is—Hic si frena remiserit, &c. (ɪɪ viii. 16). 74. 25, se ilca forwyrnð ðærre sæ ðæt heo ne mot ðone ðeorsewold oferstæppan ðæres corðan,—notice the fine metaphor in ‘ðeorsewold ðære corðan,’ which is not contained in the original—Ut fluctus avidum mare Certo fine coerceat Ne terris liceat vagis Latos tendere terminos (ɪɪ viii. 9).

76. 6, ða hæfde he me gebunden mid ðære wynnsumnesse his sanges,—the trope is slightly different in the Latin—cum me audiendi avidum stupentemque arrectis adhuc auribus carminis mulcedo defixerat. 76. 17, ymbe ðone læcedom ðara ðinra lara hwene mare gehyran,—the Latin has merely—remedia . . . audiendi avidus (ɪɪɪ i. 7). 76. 28, hwile se læceeræft is minre lare . . . se is swiðe biter on muðe and he ðe tirð on ða ðrotan ðonne ðu his ærest fandast. Ac he werodað syððan he innað and bið swiðe liðe on ðam innoðe and swiðe swete to bealcetenne,—the Latin more condensed is—ut degustata quidem mordeant, interius autem recepta dulcescant. 78. 33, gif ðu ærest awyrtwalest of ðinum mode ða leasan gesælða and hi ofatihst of ðone grund,—the trope of the Latin is quite different—Tu quoque falsa tuens bona prius Incipe colla jugo retrahere (ɪɪɪ i. 11). 84. 33, hit [Mod] bið mid ðam hwilum oferdrenced,—a continuation of the trope in the simile of the preceding context, translated from the Latin (ɪɪɪ ii. 51). 88. 3, mid ðam bridlum his anwealdes,—Quantas rerum flectat habenas Natura potens (ɪɪɪ ii. 1). 88. 5, he hi hæfð geheaðorade and gehæfte mid his unanbindendlicum racentum,—to which the Latin corresponds in sense—Stringatque ligans inreso-

luto Singula nexu (III ii. 4). 94. 22, hwæðer nu se anweald
hæbbe ðone ðeaw ðæt he astificige unðeawas and awyrtwalige of
riera manna mode and plantige ðær cræftas on,—ut utentium
mentibus virtutes inserant vitia depellant (III iv. 3); the metaphor
of the Latin just quoted is continued in 94. 24, se corðlica anweald
næfre ne sæwð ða cræftas ac lisð and gadrað unðeawas, and ðonne
hi gegadrad hæfð, ðonne cowað he hi nalles ne hilð. 118. 33, ða
sceadra ðære soðan gesælðe,—from which the Latin slightly differs
—formam felicitatis (III viii. 1). 132. 29, ofenum eagum ures Modes
we moten gescon ðone æðelan æwelm ealra goda,—of which only
the latter trope is in the Latin—Da fontem lustrare boni (III ix. 23).
132. 31, Forgif us ðonne hale eagan ures Modes ðæt we hi ðonne
moton afæstnian on ðe,—to which—da luce reperta In te con-
spicuos animi defigere visus (III ix. 23). 132. 32, todrif ðone
mist ðe nu hangað beforan ures Modes eagum,—Dissice terrenæ
nebulas et pondera molis (III ix. 25). 132. 33, onliht ða eagan
mid ðinum leohte, forðam ðu eart sio birhtu ðæs soðan leohtes,—
which is an expansion of the Latin—tuo splendore mica (III ix. 25).

132. 34, ðu eart seo softe ræst soðfæstra,—corresponding exactly
to the Latin—Tu requies tranquilla piis (III ix. 26). 132. 37, ðu
eart ægðer ge weg ge ladðeow geo sio stop ðe se weg to ligð,—to
which the Latin—te cernere finis Principium vector dux semita
terminus idem (III ix. 27). 140. 2, is an God se is stemn and
staðol ealra goda. 144. 27, ðæt is sio an ræst ealra urra geswinca,
sio an hyð byð simle smyltu æfter eallum ðam ystum and ðam
yðum urra geswinca,—to which the original—Hæc erit vobis
requies laborum, Hic portus placida manens quiete Hoc pateus
unum miseris asylum (III x. 4). 144. 24, seðe nu gehæft sie mid
ðære unnyttan lufe ðisse middangeardes, sece him freodom hu he
mæge becuman to ðam gesælðum,—the Latin is more ornate in its
metaphor—Quos ligat fallax roseis catenis Terrenas habitans libido
mentes (III x. 2). 144. 29, ðæt is seo an friðstow and sio an
frofer erminga æfter ðam ermðum ðisses andweardan lifes,—note
the literal and metaphorical expressions in the same sentence; only
the latter exists in the Latin—Hoc patens unum miseris asylum
(III x. 6). 144. 32, ne onlihtað hi nauht ðæs modes eagan, ne
heora scearpnesse nauht gebetað to ðære sceawunge ðære soðan
gesælðe, ac get swiðor he ablendað ðæs modes eagan,—correspond-

ing to the terser Latin—Inlustrent aciem magisque cæcos In snas condunt animos tenebras (iii x. 11). 146. 2, mid hluttrum eagum his modes,—this expression which occurs frequently in the A. S. is generally not found in the Latin. 156. 1, mid ðam gedwolmiste his fortio ðæt hit ne mæg swa beorhte scinan swa hit wolde,— the Latin is more vivid—quod atra texit erroris nubes (iii xi. 7). 156. 2, bi𝐝 simle corn ðære soðfæstnesse sæd on ðære sawle wuni- gende,—to which—Hæret profecto semen introrsum veri (iii xi. 11). 158. 1, gif he hi ne bunde mid his unabindendlicum racentum,— a frequent expression in A. S. 158. 9, ðu eart nu fulneah cumen innon ða ceastre ðære soðan gesælðe,—the Latin is somewhat different, and may have been misunderstood by the A. S. trans- lator—ut felicitatis compos patriam sospes revisas (iii xii. 26). 158. 27, ic hæbbe funden duru ðær ðær ic ær geseat ane lytle cynan swa ðæt ic ungeaðe mihte gesecon swiðe lytellne sciman leohtes of ðisum ðeostrum,—not in the original. 164. 2, ðæt ðær aspringe sum spearca up soðfæstnesse,—to which the Latin— veritatis scintilla dissiliat (iii xii. 68). 164. 13, lætst me hider and ðider on swa ðiene wudu ðæt ic ne mæg ut arædian,—the Latin has a slightly different metaphor—Ludisne . . . me inextri- cabilem labyrinthum rationibus texens (iii xii. 77). 160. 14, God æghwær wealt mid ðam helman and mid ðam stiorroðre his godnesse,—corresponding to the Latin—omnia bonitatis clavo gubernare jure credatur (iii xii. 45), so 164. 27,—corresponding to (iii xii. 88). 166. 25, ðe mæg gesecon ðone hluttran æwellm ðæs hehstan godes and of him selfum aweorpan mæg ða ðiostro his Modes,—only the first metaphor is found in the Latin—Felix qui potuit boni Fontem visere lucidum (iii xii. 1).

170. 16, helle ðiostra to flionne and to ðæs soðes godes liohte to cumenne,—not corresponding to the Latin—Quicumque in superum diem Mentem ducere quæritis (iii xii. 53). 170. 28, ðu [Wisdom] eart Boda and forrynel ðæs soðan leohtes,—the Latin has merely—veri prævia luminis (iv i. 5). 172. 31, ic sceal ærest ðin mod gefiðerian, ðæt hit mæge hit ðy eð up ahebban ær ðon hit fleogan onginne on ða heahnesse, &c.,—so the Latin—pinnas etiam tuæ menti quibus se in altum tollere possit adfigam (iv i. 33). 174. 1, sitte him on minum hrædwæne, ðocrige him on minne weg, ic beo his latðiow,—to which—ut perturbatione

depulsa sospes in patriam meo ductu mea semita meis etiam
vehiculis revertaris (IV i. 35).   174. 6, ic nu moste ðin Mod
gefiðerigan mid ðam fiðerum,—to which—Quas [pinnas] sibi cum
velox mens induit (IV i. 3).   174. 18, se gemetgað ðone bridel
and ðæt wealdleðer ealles ymbhweorftes heofenes and eorðan,—
corresponding to the briefer Latin—orbis que habenas temperat
(IV i. 20).   174. 20, se stiorð ðam hrædwæne eallra gesceafta,—
so the Latin—volucrem currum stabilis regit (IV i. 21).   174. 26,
ða unrihtwisan cyninga and ealle ða ofermodan rican bion swiðe
unmihtige and swiðe earme wreccan,—note the brevity and terseness of the Latin—cernes tyrannos exules (IV i. 30).   180. 5, mid
hu hefigne racentum dysiges and ungesælða hi sint gebundene.
180. 33, swongornes hi ofsit and hi mid slæwðe ofercymð and
gitsung hi ablent,—notice the personification.   This does not correspond to the Latin; 'ablent' is suggested probably by 'ignorantiæ
cæcitate' (IV ii. 89).   186. 20, ðonne wynð ðæt Mod beswungen
mid ðam welme ðære hatheortnesse,—notice the mixed metaphor.
The translation is a very free one of the Latin—Hinc flagellat ira
mentem fluctus turbida tollens (IV ii. 7).   188. 1, on hu ðiostrum
horoscaðe ðara undeawa ða yfelwillendan sticiað,—note the force
of the A. S. metaphor, more expressive than the abstract idea of
the Latin—quanto in cæno probra volvantur (IV iii. 1).   188. 21, se
beah godes edleanes,—corresponding to the Latin—sapienti tamen
corona non decidet (IV iii. 14).   206. 1, swa bioð ða synfullan
Mod ablend mid heora yfelan willan, ðæt hi ne magon gesion ðæt
lioht ðære beorhtan soðfæstnesse,—to which the Latin—nequeunt
enim oculos tenebris assuetos ad lucem perspicuæ veritatis adtollere
(IV iv. 89).

206. 6, ða ablendan mod,—and similarly 206. 20, ðæt ælc mon
sie ablend swa hi sint,—and 206. 26, ðæs Modes eagan weorðan
swa ablende.   210. 3, ðæt mon ðær mæge sniðan and bærnan
his undeawas,—for which the Latin supplies the idea of prun-
ing—ut culpæ morbos supplicis resecarent (IV iv. 129).   210. 9,
ænigne spearcan wisdomes hæfdon,—which translates the Latin
—si eis aliqua rimula virtutem relictam fas esset aspicere (IV
iv. 133).   210. 27, gebidan gecyndelices deaðes, nu he cow ælce
dæg towcardes onet,—note the personification, contained more
vividly in the Latin—si mortem petitis, propinquat ipsa Sponte sua

volucres nec remoratur equos (IV iv. 3); so also 210. 28, hwi ne
magon ge gesion ðæt he spyra𝛿 . . . æfter monnum and ne forlæt
nan swieð ær he gefehð ðæt ðæt he æfter syreð. 218. 18, ac
God wunað simle on ðære hean ceastre his anfealdnesse and bile-
witnesse,—the Latin, referring to the mind of God, has—Hæc in
suæ simplicitatis arce composita (IV vi. 24). 226. 18, hwæt is
sawla hælo bute rihtwisnes; oððe hwæt is hiora untrumnes bute
unðeawas. Hwa is ðonne betera læce ðære sawle ðonne . . .
God,—to which the Latin—Quid vero aliud animorum salus vide-
tur esse quam probitas? quid ægritudo quam vitia? quis autem
alius vel servator bonorum vel malorum depulsor quam rector ac
medicator mentium deus? (IV vi. 112); so 230. 17, ac se goda
læce, ðæt is God, lacnað hiora Mod mid ðam welan,—the Latin
does not mention God—hujus morbo providentia collatæ pecuniæ
remedio medetur (IV vi. 163). 232. 21, hit [song] is se læcedom
and se drenc, ðe ðu lange wilnodest,—the Latin has only—haustum
quo refectus firmior in ulteriora contendas (IV vi. 199). 234. 22,
ðanon he welt ðam gewealdleðerum calle gesceaftu,—so the Latin
—Rerumque regens flectit habenas (IV vi. 35). 240. 18, hit is
swa fyrn of uncrum wege, of ðæm wege ðe wit getiohhod habbað
on to farenne,—to which the Latin—hæc autem etsi perutilia
cognitu tamen a propositi nostri tramite paulisper aversa sunt
verendumque est, ne deviis fatigatus ad emetiendum rectum iter
sufficere non possis (V i. 9). 246. 23, wadað on hiora agenne
willan and æfter hiora lichoman luste irnað. 254. 17, ðæt ðu
mæge . . . cumon . . . to ðinre agenre cyððe ðonne ðu ær come,—
transferred to a spiritual sense. 256. 12, habban ær ðines modes
eagan clæne and hluttre.

The metaphor of Anglo-Saxon poetry is bolder and more spon-
taneous than that of the prose. Poetry itself had reached a stage
of development never attained by prose, and it is only natural that
such rhetorical features as the tropes should be more effectively
employed in an advanced poetry than in an incipient prose.
Further, from the very subject of this prose, there was not such
a demand for figurative speech. The prose, for the most part, was
written with a didactic purpose. The style must necessarily be
simple. Only such metaphorical language may be used as will

be readily understood by the masses. When the homilist uses a metaphor which may be obscure, he often interprets it, with the result, however, that, while he makes its meaning unmistakable, he often robs it of all its force. The imaginative metaphors of poetry would tend to obscure the preacher's message. Consequently, all his metaphors are simple and direct, and are for the most part taken from the most familiar experiences of life, whether they come from literature or the casual observation of daily phenomena. Originality is not one of the features of this metaphor. The Scriptures and the Church Fathers used the simplest tropes forcibly to express their thoughts, and the A. S. homilist, satisfied with their fitness for his purpose, adopted them with only such change as rendered them more intelligible to his audience.

Considerable literary skill was frequently shown in the adaptation of these tropes to Anglo-Saxon conditions. For instance, Christ is spoken of in the New Testament as the light of the world ; Ælfric, with his A. S. horror of darkness, treats the metaphor as follows : "Crist is se soða dæg, seðe todræfde mid his tocyme ealle nytennysse ðære ealdan nihte, and ealne middangeard mid his gife onlihte."[1] All metaphors relating to war, the sea, the feast, etc., would be easily adopted by the homilist, and would readily appeal to the instincts of the people. Thus, " mid deofles flan ðurhscotene,"[2] compares not unfavourably with the Biblical "fiery darts of the wicked."[3] So the relation of master and servant is well employed in "ne bið he ðæra æhta *hlaford*, ðonne he hi dælan ne mæg ; ac he bið ðæra æhta *ðeowa*, ðonne he him callunga ðeowað."[4] The intense A. S. dread of banishment adds great force to the metaphor,—" we ealle sind *cuman* on ðisum life, and *ure eard* nis na her ; ac we sind her swilce wegferende men."[5] The Biblical " rooted and grounded in love "[6] apparently suggests the metaphor of " heora heortan wyrtruman on his lufes aplantodon."[7] Wulfstan shows considerable vigour in " ðæt deofol ne mæg ænig his ættrenra wæpna him on afæstnjan "[8] and in " flyhð se frofur aweg,"[9] but his metaphors are comparatively few.

---

[1] A. II. 36. 28.

[2] A. II. 62. 14.

[3] *Ephes.* vi. 16.

[4] A. II. 66. 6.

[5] A. H. 248. 14.

[6] *Ephes.* iii. 17.

[7] A. H. 612. 29.

[8] B. H. 35. 17.

[9] B. H. 139. 13.

His rhetorical devices are confined for the most part to the figures of euphony. Ælfric varies in his use of the metaphor; in the first part of the first volume there are a large number, but in the remaining homilies they are less frequent. The same is true of the Blickling Homilies; the first ten homilies have many more than the rest of the collection.

The point of view from which the metaphor of the Boethius is treated must necessarily be different from that of the homiletic metaphor. While the homilists were more or less influenced by ecclesiastical literature, their work was, in a way, original; but in the present instance we have to deal with a direct translation. The translation is by no means exact. Alfred, the reputed translator, in his preface (viii. 2), says: "Sometimes he set word by word, sometimes meaning of meaning, as he most plainly and clearly could explain it for the various and manifold worldly occupations which often busied him both in mind and body."

An examination into the originality of the metaphors of the Boethius gives the following results. Of the 130 metaphors quoted above, 70 are more or less literal translations of the original, which preserve the metaphorical idea intact. That only about half the metaphors of a translation should belong to the original shows the great freedom which the translator exercised. Of those remaining, 35 have no exact correspondents in the Latin; there are nine cases in which there is a change in the metaphorical idea from the original to the translation, eleven cases in which the trope is suggested by the immediate context of the Latin, and five cases where literal statement is translated by figurative.

If we examine the original metaphors of this translation, we shall find that they show a decided superiority to the average metaphor of the homilies. Not that the figurative ideas are more striking or original than such as we find in all the homilies, but the general average is higher. What occurs only in isolated instances in the homilies is the norm in the Boethius. The ideas are such as are easily suggested by the environments of the writer and do not in themselves indicate any especial keenness of observation. The merit of these metaphors consists in their variety and their appropriateness to the context. A new vigour is given the exhausted trope by the terseness and not unfrequent brevity of the expression. The allegorical interpretation is not so frequent nor so elaborate.

The metaphors which are classed as translations are not, by any means, literal. The translator always felt at liberty to treat the Latin as he chose, and when, in the 70 cases mentioned, he adopted the figurative idea of the original, he gave it what expression he pleased. Sometimes he surpasses the Latin, at other times he does not.

The instances of the substitution of a metaphorical for a literal statement are rare, and are such as, to the A. S. mind, have almost lost their colour; thus ' hrof' for ' summum,' ' fleon ' for ' abeat,' etc.

The cases where a change of the figurative idea occurs are due often to a desire on the part of the translator to avoid any obscurity of reference in the Latin. Thus the Latin Sirenes, a metaphorical expression for temptations and cares, is translated by the less vivid A. S. sceaðan,[1] because Sirenes would suggest nothing to the Anglo-Saxon mind; in 164. 13, ðiene wudu occurs for inextricabilem labyrinthum, a translation that retains all the force of the original and presents no possible obscurity.

The remaining metaphors are those suggested by the context of the originals. The same trope will occur sometimes in two places in the Anglo-Saxon, where there is only one in the Latin; or a trope, not translated in its original context, is used elsewhere. Again, as in 180. 33, gitsung hi ablent, where the metaphor is evidently suggested by the Latin ignorantiæ cæcitate, the Anglo-Saxon is not a translation, but is suggested from the immediate context of the Latin.

If we look through the lists collected by Professor Gummere, we shall learn the essential character of the metaphor of poetry. The following illustrations will, perhaps, suffice for illustration :— D. 442, healme hrof heofona rices, 'the sky'; E. 287, famge feldas, 'the sea'; B. 1143, hildeleoman . . . on bearm dyde, 'thrust a sword into his breast'; B. 1032, fela lafe, 'the swords,'—lafe is "applied to weapons, escaped persons, the seashore, etc."[2] G. 2145, æðelinga helm, 'the leader of the nobles'; G. 1608, breosta hord, 'life.' These are metaphorical expressions for very commonplace

---

[1] 4. 23.   [2] Gummere. p. 33.

ideas, and indicate the picturesqueness of the poetic speech in contrast to the unadorned prose. This is but one of the significant distinctions between prose and poetry. "The typical A. S. metaphor [of poetry] was originally confined to one word, or at the furthest, to several words that stood in the closest syntactical relation."[1] In this respect the prose differs somewhat, since it does not have that terseness of phrase which marks the poetry. Though the elaborated metaphor appears only in the form of the allegorical interpretation, where the metaphor can hardly be said to have an independent existence, there are many instances where the trope is expanded beyond the limits noted in the poetic metaphor. Sustained carrying on of a single figurative idea is rare; the author prefers to fall back on literal statement, often mixing the two up in a rather incongruous fashion, or to run into simile, or spring to another figurative idea in the form of a metaphor or a simile.

2. SIMILE.

The definition of Simile in the *Century Dictionary* is "the comparing or likening of two things having some strong point or points of resemblance, both of which are mentioned and the comparison directly stated; a poetic or imaginative comparison; also a verbal expression or embodiment of such a comparison."

A. H.

6. 1, ðæt his gecorenan ðegenas beon aclænsode fram callum synnum ðurh ða ormatan ehtnyssa, swa swa gold bið on fyre afandod, so 268. 14, 544. 6 ; 64. 14, ðæt ge to lytelre hwile scinon swa swa rose, ðæt ge hrædlice forweornion ; 144. 11, swa swa leoht todræfð ðeostra swa eac todræfð Cristes lufu . . . ealle leohtras and synna fram ure heortan ; 154. 17, nis heo hwæðere ðe · gelicere ðære ecan worulde, ðe is sum cwearteru leohtum dæge ; 182. 31, rihtlice is seo sæ wiðmeten ðisre worulde, forðon ðe heo is hwiltidum smylte and myrige on to rowenne, hwilon eac hreoh and egeful on to beonne. Swa is ðeos woruld, etc.,— the homilist proceeds to interpret his trope. 184. 33, seo miht

---

[1] Gummere, p. 53.

wæs ða on Cristes handum and ða fif hlafas wæron swylce hit sæd wære, na on eorðan besawen, ac gemenigfyld fram ðam ðe eorðan geworhte; 248. 15, we sind her swilce wegferende menn,—the impressive reference to the misery of exile. 268. 25, he fierð swa him deofol wissað, swa swa tobrocen scip on sæ, ðe swa fierð swa hit se wind drifð; 274. 6, se ðe ðe mundað swa swa fæder, he bið swylce he ðin heafod sy; 296. 27, swa swa fyr forniinð wæteres dropan, swa fornam Cristes godcundlice miht ðone geðigedan mete; 312. 20, ure ehteras beoð besencte ðurh ðæt halige fulluht swa swa wæs Pharao . . . in ðære Readan Sæ; 354. 33, he wæs asend toforan Drihtne swa swa se dægsteorra gæð beforan ðære sunnan, swa swa bydel ætforan deman, swa swa seo calde gecyðnys ætforan ðære niwan,—the meanness of the two last similes is in striking contrast to the beauty of the first. 356. 1, seo ealde æ wæs swilce sceadu; 362. 22, swa swa wæter scyt of ðære dune and ætstent on dune, swa forflihð se Halga Gast modigra manna heortan; 444. 31, his ðrowung swa swa swurd ðurhferde hire sawle; 456. 23, his stemn is swylce ormæte byme; 472. 15, se læce cyrfð oððe bærnð and se untruma hrymð, ðeahhwæðere ne miltsað he ðæs oðres wanunge, forðan gif se læce geswicð his cræftes, ðonne losað se forwundoda. Swa eac God gelaenað his gecorena gyltas mid mislicum brocum, etc.,—with an elaboration of the idea as applied to the spiritual life. 492. 32, ðonne he bið mid idelan hlisan . . . befangen, ðonne bið hit swylce he sy mid sumere moldhlipan ofhroren; 526. 19, on ðyssere andwerdan gelaðunge sind gemengde yfele and gode, swa swa clæne corn mid fulum coccele; 544. 7, swa swa halige offrunga hi underfeng to his heofonlican rice; 592. 11, mannes ege is smice gelic and hrædlice, ðonne he astyred bið, forwinð; 602. 12, symle hnesce beon on urum geleafan, swa swa ðas merwan cild; 614. 10, ðes middangeard is ðam caldigendan menn gelic,—an elaborate enumeration of the details of resemblance is entered upon, and carried on with considerable skill.

A. H. ii.

258. 11, ðæt Judeisc folc wæs on ealdum dagum Gode gecoren, swa swa god win; ac hi wurdon awende to ðam wyrstum ecede;

300. 30, an steorra stod, se wæs swurde gelic . . . beorhte scynende; 352. 3, æteowode min lattcow swa swa scinende steorra; 380. 9, wyle hine aðwean mid wope fram synnum, and eft hine befylan fullice mid leahtrum swa swa swyn deð, ðe cyrð to meoxe æfter his ðweale,—notice the metaphor in the first clause. Cf. II Peter ii. 22. 392. 21, behealdað ðæs woruld swa swa sæ,—elaborated to considerable length by the comparison of Peter's attempt to walk on the sea and his consequent failure with the experiences of man on the sea of life. 446. 31, swa stod se deofol on Godes gesihðe swa swa deð se blinda on sunnan; 488. 27, hi [the magicians] ðotorodon swilce oðre wulfas; 530. 20, Hilarium . . . Scinende swa swa tungel on soðre lare; 532. 9, ne sceal he teran ne bitan swa swa wulf; 536. 19, swa swa sealt hylt ælcne mete wið forrotodnysse, swa sceal ðæs wisdomes bodung healdan manna heortan wið brosnunge fulra leahtra; 590. 7, hi farað ðurh ðæt fyr to Criste buton ælcere dare, swilce hi on sunnan leoman faron,—this can hardly be called a simile; compare, however, Dan. 275, ac wæs ðær inne ealles gelicost efne ðonne on sumera sunne scineð, and deawdrias on dæge weorðeð, winde geondsawen. 602. 25, se man ðe æfter ðædbote his manfullan dæda geedniwað, se gegremeð God and he bið ðam hunde gelic ðe spiwð and eft ett ðæt ðæt he ær aspaw,—cf. II Peter ii. 22.

W. H.

149. 4, swa læne ys oferlufu eorðan gestreona; efnes hit bið gelic rena scurum, ðonne hi nyðer of heofonum swyðost dreosað and eft raðe call toglidað, ðonne bið fæger wider and beorht sunne; 150. 5, ne mæg se preost ænigum synfullum men wel dædbote tæcan ær he gehyre his synne ðe ma, ðe ænig læce mæg ænigne untrumne man wel læcnjan, ær he hæbbe ðæt attor ut aspiwan; 234. 28, he [the wicked soul] bið wyrsa ðonne hund oððe æninges cynnes nyten, ðonne he into cyrcan cymð; 238. 5, swa swa wæter adwæsceð fyr, swa adwæsceð seo ælmesse ða synne; 241. 6, ðu [sin] wære swa gifre swa hund and ðu næfre nære full ðe ma, ðe hell; 257. 20, efne hit bið gelic, ðæt man mid wætere ðone weallendan welm ofgeote, ðæt he leng ne mot rixjan swa man mid ælmessan synna ealle alyseð; 262. 5, ðæt

treow ðonne, ðe wexeð on ðam wudubearme, ðæt hit hlifað up
ofer eall ða oðre treowu and brædeð hit, ðonne semninga storm
gestandeð and se stranga wind, ðonne bið hit swiðlicor geweged
and gesweneged, ðonne se oðer wudu. Swa bið eac gelice be ðam
beaclifum and teorrum, ðonne hi hlifjað feor up ofer ða oðre
eorðan, hy ðonne semninga feallan onginnað and full ðearlice
hreosan to eorðan. Swylce eac be ðam hean muntum and
dunum . . . Swa ða hean mihta her on worulde hreosað and
feallað and to lore weorðað, and ðisse worulde welan weorðað
to sorge, and ðas corðlican wunder weorðað to nahte; 264. 1,
hit [love of riches] bið gelic rena scurum, ðonne hy of heofenum
swiðost dreosað and eft hraðe eall toglidað.

B. H.

21. 26, hwyle bið he [the body] ðonne buton swylce stan oððe
treow; 29. 32, englas beoð aa halgum mannum on fultume swa
swa scyld; 57. 34, hwyle se deadlica lichama bið, ðonne seo
saul of bið, and seo fægernes ðe he her on worlde lufode, swyle
ðes blowenda wudu and ðas blowendan wyrta; 59. 19, ealle ða
gewitað swa swa wolcn and swa swa wæteres stream; 59. 28, eal
swylce seo lange mettrumnes bið ðæs seocan mannes, ðonne hine
God forlætan nele eðelice lifian, ne he ðeah swyltan ne mote, and
swa ðeah hwæðere oð ðone deað he hine tintregað, swyle is
ðæt lif ðysses middangeardes; 87. 30, ic gedwolede swa swa ðæt
sceap ðæt forwearð; 89. 9, ic wæs wiðermede and unwisum
netenum gelic geworden; 91. 35, heofon bið gefealden swa swa
boc; 109. 36, se flæschoma ascyred swa glæs; 137. 30, swiðe
scinende palmtwig and hit wæs ða swa leoht swa se mergenlica
steorra; 147. 16, heo hæfde scofon siðum beorhtran saule ðonne
snaw, so 147. 27; 203. 9, ða flugon ða legetu swylce fyrene
strælas ongean ða hæðnan leode; 209. 36, ða fynd ðara on uiera
onlicnesse heora gripende wæron, swa swa grædig wulf; 237. 6,
ðin blod flewð ofer eorðan swa swa wæter, so 241. 27.

BOETH.

14. 24, ða sæ ðe ær wæs smylte wedere glæshlutru on to seonne,
—to which the Latin is, Vitrea dudum Parque serenis Unda diebus

(I vii. 8). 22. 3, ac ðonne ic up gefare mid ðinum ðeowum, ðonne forseo we ðas styrmendan woruld, swa se earn ðonne he up gewit bufan ða wolcnu styrmendum wederum ðæt him ða stormas derian ne mahan,—this fine simile is not found in the Latin. 36. 12, swa swa sigende sond ðonne ren swylgð, swa swylgð seo gitsung ða dreosendan welan ðisses middangeardes, forðam heo hiora simle bið ðurstegu,—not in the original. 48. 19, manna gitsung is swa byrnende swa ðæt fyr on ðære helle, se is on ðam munte ðe Ætne hatte,—from which the Latin differs in expression but not in the idea, Sed sævior ignibus Ætnæ Fervens amor ardet habendi (II v. 25). 50. 3, calle ða rieu . . . forslean and forheregian swa swa fyres lig deð dryne hæð feld oððe eft se byrnenda swefl ðone munt . . . Ætne,—the simile is wanting in the Latin, but the idea, as embodied in the A. S., is found: quæ si in improbissimum quemque ceciderunt, quæ flammis Ætnæ eructuantibus, quod diluvium tantas strages dederint (II vi. 4). 72. 4, seo orsorhnes græð scyrmælum swa ðæs windes yst,—the Latin has not the simile,—itaque illam videas ventosam fluentem suique semper ignaram (II viii. 13). 72. 9, seo wiðerweardnes . . . getihð to ðam soðum gesælðum swa swa mid angle fisc gefangen bið,—not in the Latin. 80. 23, swa swa ealle cumað of ðære sæ and eft ealle cumað to ðære sæ,—this simile, describing the greatest happiness, is not found in the Latin. 84. 30, swa swa oferdruncen man wat ðæt he sceolde to his huse and to his ræste and ne mæg ðeah ðider aredian, swa bið eac ðam Mode, ðonne hit bið ahefigad mid ðæm ymbhogum ðisse worulde,— veluti ebrius domum quo tramite revertatur ignorat (III ii. 51). 90. 3, Eala, hwæt ge eorðlican men, ge eow selfe nu don neatum gelice for eowre dysige,—the simile is only implied in the Latin, vos quoque O terrena animalia tenui licet (III iii. 1). 98. 18, ðis andwearde lif is swiðe anlic sceade and on ðære sceade nan mon ne mæg begitan ða soðan gesælða,—an expansion of a mere suggestion in the Latin, per umbrabiles dignitates (III iv. 28). So, probably, is suggested the following: 98. 31, hi lociað swa swa scealdu oððe smec. 112. 26, swa swa seo beo sceal losian, ðonne heo hwæt yrringa stingð, swa sceal ælce sawl forweorðan æfter ðam unrihthamede,—the idea is not found in the Latin of the death of the bee, but the popular belief is suggested by the mere mention of the bee's sting.   The Latin is—

> Habet omnis hoc voluptas
> Stimulis agit fruentes
> Apiumque par volantum,
> Ubi grata mella fudit
> Fugit et nimis tenaci
> Ferit icta corda morsu (III vii.).

116. 17, se wlite ðæs lichoman is . . . swiðe anlic eorðan blost-mum,—corresponding closely to the Latin, Formæ vero nitor ut rapidus est ut velox et vernalium florum mutabilitate fugacior (III vii. 20). 132. 21, sume [souls] beorhtor . . . swa swa steorran, ælc be his gelarnunga. 134. 9, sum god . . . sie ðæt hehste, swa swa sum micel æwelm and deop and irnon manige brocas and riðan of,—the Latin is much terser, hoc veluti quidam omnium fons bonorum (III x. 8).   154. 2, ðæt ealle gesceafta tofleowon swa swa wæter,—the Latin is, et uno veluti vertice destituta sine rectore fluitabunt (III xi. 108).   158. 24, he is ana staðolfæst wealdend and steora and steorroðor, forðæm he reht and ðæt eallum gesceaftum, swa swa god steora anum scipe,— so the Latin, hic est veluti quidam clavus atque gubernaculum quo mundana machina stabilis . . . servatur (III xii. 38).   172. 11, wisdom and eac oðre cræftas . . . licgað forsewene swa swa meox under feltune,—how vivid the simile renders the thought, expressed metaphorically in the Latin, virtus . . . sceleratorum pedibus subjecta calcatur et in locum facinorum supplicio luit (IV i. 15).   188. 2, hu ða godan scinað beorhtor ðonne sunne,— the Latin wants the simile, qua probitas luce resplendeat (IV iii. 2). 192. 26, he bið anlicost fettum swinum, ðe simle willnað licgan on fulum solum,—the Latin expresses it more briefly as a meta-phor, sordidæ suis voluptate detinetur (IV iii. 63).   196. 31, se yfela willa bið tostenced swa se recels beforan fyre,—not in the Latin.   198. 8, ac swiðe oft se micla anweald ðara yfelena gehrist swiðe færlice, swa swa great beam on wyda wyrcð hludne dynt ðonne men læst wenað,—an expressive simile not in the original. 204. 1, and ða amarod on ðam heofonlicum fyre swa her bið sylfor,—the simile is not in the Latin.   210. 24, forhwi drefe ge

3

eowre mod mid unrihtre fiounge, swa swa yða for winde ða sæ
hrerað,—the only suggestion in the Latin is, Quid tantos juvat
excitare Motus (IV iv. 1).   216. 28, buton he hæbbe swa scearp
andget swa ðæt fyr,—corresponding to the metaphor of the Latin,
vivacissimo mentis igne (IV vi. 10).   228. 11, se godcunda anweald gefriðode his diorlingas under his fiðera sceade and hi
scilde swa geornlice swa swa man deð ðone æpl on his eagan.
Cf. *Ps.* xvii. 8.

The position of the Simile in A. S. Poetry is thus stated by
Professor Gummere:[1] "The Simile . . . is very sparely repre-
sented in A. S. Poetry.   It is in opposition to the general tone,
and requires a balance, a mastery of the subject, that is not to be
looked for when, as in the best poems, the subject masters the
singer.   Well known exceptions to this rule are such passages as
occur in Cynewulf's *Crist*, in the *Panther*, in the *Phœnix*, etc.,
and are all easily detected imitations of foreign models."

Referring to the presence of the Simile in Modern English,
Professor Earle[2] says that "it is comparatively rare in prose;
its proper field is Epic Poetry."   Professor Gummere's investigations show how different, in this regard, the Epic Poetry of
Anglo-Saxon is from that of Modern English; in the prose, we
do not find such a difference.   It is manifest from the above lists
how much fewer the similes are than the metaphors.   And when
we consider, as Professor Earle further remarks, that "it is in the
sermon perhaps more than in any other form of literature that we
may find specimens of the figured diction, which is requisite to
find the highest order of prose,"[3] we realize how foreign must
have been the Simile to the genius of the language.

There is something in the very nature of the Simile which
would account for its comparative infrequency.   To quote Professor Earle again:[4] "Similes and pictured ideas are sought out
for the sake of ornament, but Metaphor is a resource of expression
that starts up instinctively by affinity with the process of sincere

[1] *A. S. Met.*, p. 52.   [2] John Earle: *English Prose;* London, 1890, p. 235.
[3] *Ibid.*, p. 236.   [4] *Ibid.*, p. 239.

meditation." There is a distinct consciousness of elaboration in the Simile, a worked out statement of figurative resemblances, which we do not find in the Metaphor. In a primitive literature such as the Anglo-Saxon, we should not, accordingly, expect the Simile to be so highly developed.

The Anglo-Saxons had not reached that stage in their development of prose where they could treat the Simile as a means of ornamentation. It was foreign to the language, and was adopted from the Christian literature, where it had been flourishing for centuries. The ornamentation which the Anglo-Saxons did employ was in the figures of euphony, which were familiar to them from immemorial use in their poetry. We shall see later how extensively they transferred these figures from poetry to prose. A rhetorical device is not likely to be elaborated unless it is part of the genius of the language; that which is borrowed will be used sparingly, and only those which are the special property of the language will lend themselves to elaboration. The lists from the prose but confirm the conclusions reached from the much scantier instances of the poetry, that the Simile is not a natural product of Anglo-Saxon soil, but is an importation from the fertile fields of the Ecclesiastical Latin.

The Simile is also of infrequent occurrence in the *Boethius*. Of the 27 instances quoted above, there are ten not suggested by the Latin, and these are all very good. The remainder more or less faithfully translate the text of the Latin, with the preservation of the figured idea, or they obtain the simile from the immediate context. Of the former there are eight, of the latter nine. The Anglo-Saxon may have a simile where the Latin has a metaphor, or it may expand to some length the idea contained in one word of its original.

It is interesting to note the sustained similes, as A. H. 614. 10, A. H. II 392. 21, W. H. 262. 5, B. H. 59. 28. Such a type is to be regarded as due to the influence of the allegorical interpretation, into which a simile or metaphor frequently merges.

What has been said of the sources of the ideas in the Metaphor applies with equal truth to the Simile. The Scriptures, the Fathers, and the common experiences of life furnished all the figurative needs of these writers. We do not meet with many

similes which arrest our attention by their originality; some
of them are of considerable excellence and are not on the whole
inferior to the metaphors, but the vital quality of the trope of
poetry is always wanting. Anglo-Saxon prose is never great,
its rhetorical devices never brilliant; its aim was to teach the
people by means of the direct homily; its writers were earnest
preachers, not men of great literary genius.

II. PHONETIC OR SOUND-FIGURES.

Under the head of Phonetic Figures, Gerber remarks[1] that
there are three kinds. The first endeavours to embody in the
name of an object a sound corresponding to its sense; the second
kind disregards the meaning, considers the sound only, and
arranges this sound in such an order that a musical effect is
produced in speech; the third kind employs the sound only as a
necessary means for definitely denoting an idea, and only so far
as it produces a rhetorical effect. The general term for the first
division is *Onomatopöie*, for the second, *Figures of Similarity in
Sound and of Euphony*, and for the third, *Word-figures*. This
treatment will deal only with the two latter groups.

1 *a.*—Figures of Similarity in Sound.

Of the various figures coming under this division, only *a.
Homoioteleuton* and *β. Paromoion* are considered here.

a. Homoioteleuton.

The *Century Dictionary* defines *Homoioteleuton* as "a figure consisting in the use of a succession of words or clauses concluding
with the same sounds.—*Note.* More comprehensive than rime,
including rime, some other forms of assonance, and all other cases
of similarity of termination in successive words, clauses, or lines."
In this treatment the figure will be limited to those cases where
compound words in close syntactic relation end in the same sound,
which includes the last member of the compound. Other cases
will be considered under *Epiphora*.

[1] II 113.

A. H.

14. 14, deor*cynn* and fugel*cynn*, so 16. 5, 20. 34, 102. 5, 488. 10; 36. 25, heofen*wara*, and eorᵹ*wara*, and hel*wara*, so ɪɪ 360. 32, 604. 5; 144. 22, an*fealdlice* hi sind scyldige . . ., and twy*fealdlice* hi beoᵹ fordemde; 148. 14, ge on wæp*mannum* ge on wif*mannum*, so 442. 1; 438. 34, in*farende* and ut*farende;* 536. 27, fram east*dæle* and fram west*dæle;* 606. 20, on scalm*sangum* and gastlicum lof*sangum*.

A. H. ɪɪ.

14. 25, on diacon*hade*, ge on preost*hade*, ge on biscop*hade*, so 564. 2; 184. 13, wunode ᵹa niht un*willes*, seᵹe sylf*willes* nolde; 536. 9, on nyᵹe*weardum* wid and on ufe*weardum* nearo, so 496. 25.

W. H.

40. 10, wed*logan* ne word*logan;* 40. 17, ofermode ne to wea*mode;* 44. 28, heofon*waru* and eorᵹ*waru;* 72. 7, seᵹe wære wea*mod*, weorᵹe se geᵹyld*mod*, seᵹe wære hoh*mod*, weorᵹe se glæd*mod;* 72. 14, seᵹe wære full *slaw*, weorᵹe se un*slaw;* 72. 16, seᵹe wære leas*sagol*, weorᵹe se soᵹ*sagol;* 72. 17, seᵹe wære stunt*wyrde*, weorᵹe se wis*wyrde;* 72. 9, seᵹe wære idel*georn*, weorᵹe se not*georn;* 82. 5, ᵹeos woruld is gemænged mid mænig*fealdan* mane and mid fela*fealdan* facne,—note the alliteration. 113. 1, freols*tida* and fæsten*tida;* 117. 14, freols*dagum* and ymbren*dagum* and lencten-*dagum* and rihtfæsten*dagum;* 129. 17, ᵹurh morᵹ*dæda* and ᵹurh man*dæda;* ᵹurh man*slihtas* and ᵹurh mæg*slihtas* . . ., ᵹurh swic-*domas* and ᵹurh un*domas*, ᵹurh had*bricas* and ᵹurh æw*bricas*, ᵹurh sib*legera* and ᵹurh mistlice for*ligru;* 130. 5, ᵹurh aᵹ*bricas* and ᵹurh wed*bricas;* 136. 4, beforan eallum heofon*warum* and eorᵹ*warum* and hel*warum*, so 202. 22; 139. 22, ges*ælig* and ofer-*sælig;* 155. 2, husl*ganges* and in*ganges;* 158. 15, freo*riht* fornum-ena and ᵹræl*riht* generwde and ælmes*riht* gewanode; 163. 21, ᵹurh morᵹ*dæda* and ᵹurh man*dæda;* 164. 4, ᵹurh had*brycas* and ᵹurh æw*brycas*, so 164. 7, 9; 164. 11, cyric*hatan* hetole and leod*hatan* grimme; 164. 5, ᵹurh sib*blegeru* and ᵹurh mistlice for*ligru;* 170. 2, orf*cwealm* oᵹᵹon man*cwealm*, so 172. 17; 203. 6,

eall heofen*wered* and eall eorð*wered* and eall hell*wered;* 232. 24,
to gebed*huse* na to nanum gemot*huse,* so 303. 1; 268. 19, ðæs
wær*scipes* and calles ðæs weorð*scipes;* 298. 14, mans*lagan* and
mægs*lagan* . . . had*brecan* and æw*brecan.*

B. H.

11. 4, heofon*ware* ge eorð*ware;* 15. 2, be ðisse ond*weardan,* ge
eac be ðære to*weardan;* 51. 35, yrfe*weardas* and last*weardas;*
79. 19, mid wif*mannum* and wæpned*mannum;* 83. 18, god*cunde*
blisse and eac world*cunde;* 93. 11, on ðæm norð-*ende* and on ðam
east-*ende;* 93. 22, from ðæm cast*dæle* to ðone west*dæl;* 217. 8,
ar*fæst* and gemet*fæst.*

In the Ælfrician and Blickling Homilies, the occurrence of
Homoioteleuton is comparatively infrequent. The instances, moreover, can hardly be said to possess any real rhetorical value; they
seem to be conventional combinations, which readily recur to
the preacher's mind. We are, however, conscious that, in such an
example as B. H. 15. 2, cited above, there is an effort to attain
rhetorical effectiveness; but these examples constitute a meagre
minority.

In several of the so-called Wulfstan Homilies, we realize a
marked difference. Here we have no doubt of the oratorical
purpose of the preacher in his use of the figure. He rises above
the conventional limits of the figure and pours forth his thought
in sentences marked by this recurring rime. It is a noticeable
feature of those homilies in which he is strongly moved. It indicates, with the figures of Rime and Assonance, the value that
these rhetorical devices must have possessed in the literary consciousness of the Anglo-Saxon, when used by such a master as
Wulfstan.

β. *Paromoion.*

Paromoion is the reverse of Homoioteleuton; it is the repetition
of the initial syllable or syllables of words in the same sentence.
The instances are very rare; no examples have been noted in
Ælfric, and very few in the Blickling Collection. Wulfstan alone
justifies us in considering the figure.

W. H.

40. 10, *manswican* and *manswor*an, so 203. 21, 274. 24; 53. 10, ongean *modsta*ðolnysse and *modes* strencðe,—this case may be allowed to pass since the last two nouns hardly differ from the first in the feeling we have for them as a compound. 57. 12, se man hæfð *wis*dom ðe *wis*lice leofað; 173. 13, mid *halig*dome . . . and mid *halig*wætere; 173. 20, se *scir*bisceop and eal *scir*witan; 309. 21, *hor*ingas and *hor*ewenan.

B. H.

45. 18, *efen*halig his apostolum and *efen*hlete his witgum; 61. 9, ðam *riht*gelyfendum monnum and *riht* dondum; 187. 29, soðfæst and soðsecgende.

1 *b*.—FIGURES OF EUPHONY.

a. Alliteration.

Alliteration is "the riming of the initial sounds of words or syllables," and in Anglo-Saxon verse " is employed to unite the two half-lines into the larger rhythmical unit of the complete line."[1] From its being a characteristic feature of poetry, it is not surprising that it should be found to a considerable extent in prose. Here, however, it must be treated with great caution, since cases of alliteration may occur in which there was no design on the part of the author; they may be merely fortuitous collocations of words with similar initial sounds.

If we consider the occurrences according to an arbitrary grouping of words in certain syntactical relations, we shall find that some combinations are more often marked by alliteration than others.

The examples under (*a*.), the Noun and its qualifying Adjective, which may be considered as intentional, are comparatively rare. The following would seem to indicate a conscious effort after this effect :

---

[1] James W. Bright: *An Anglo-Saxon Reader*, New York, 1894, p. 230.

A. H.

62. 30, on *w*uldorlicum *w*uldre ; 162. 11, *w*oruldlican *w*ur*ð*mynt ; 244. 24, *ð*æt *f*olc wæs swi*ð*e *f*yrenful ; 420. 10, *d*umba *d*eofolgyld ; 428. 6, mid *s*tearcum *s*tengum ; 446. 8, *w*ynsumestan *w*ununge ; 454. 16, *g*rimlican *g*arsecg ; 472. 6, *h*orig *h*rægl ; 472. 13, *w*oruld-lrece *w*rellhreow ; 498. 5, se *d*igla dea*ð* ; 504. 32, *f*yrenum *f*lamm ; 514. 28, *ð*wyrlican *ð*eawas ; 566. 22, saftum slæpe ; 578. 35, ure *m*odige *m*od ; 590. 10, dea*ð* is *d*eorwyr*ð*e ; 602. 15, *ð*one *s*leacan *s*leap.

A. H. II.

46. 2, so*ð*e *s*ibbe ; 120. 2, mid *w*acum *w*refelse ; 136. 30, on *s*wæcce *s*wettran ; 188. 30, *d*eopan *d*igelnysse ; 206. 18, *ð*am *d*eopan *d*ihte ; 224. 13, *m*ærlican *m*ihta ; 254. 21, *s*cyldige *s*cea*ð*an ; 410. 20, mid *s*tylre *s*temne ; 462. 24, *ð*æs *f*leogendan *f*ugelas ; 464. 16, *w*acum *w*yrtum ; 544. 19, *d*igelre *d*æde.

W. H.

14. 17, *ð*æs *m*æran *m*ædenes ; 17. 8, *f*ægere *f*or*ð*werd ; 79. 4, *l*ease *l*eogeras ; 82. 5, mid *m*ænigfealdan *m*ane and mid *f*elafealdan *f*acne ; 92. 17, *s*tyrnlice *s*tormas ; 112. 12, so*ð*e *s*ibbe and some ; 113. 5, *l*ænan *l*ife ; 139. 10, *w*ælgrimme *w*yrmas ; 146. 1, on *h*al-gum *h*ige ; 172. 2, *f*rigman swa *f*ræc sy ; 173. 15, æt *h*reocendum *h*eor*ð*e ; 190. 2, *h*alige *h*eapas ; 257. 21, *ð*one *w*eallendan *w*elm.

The examples under (*b.*), two or more Nouns in close sequence, are more numerous and are manifestly more rhetorical.

A. H.

14. 19, to *f*ultume and to *f*rofre ; 16. 2, mid his *w*isdome and mid his *w*illan ; 16. 21, he is na Scyppend ac is atelic sceocca ; 16. 24, *m*eldan and *m*anslagan ; 102. 27, on *w*æstm and on *w*an-unge ; 298. 8, *r*icum and *r*e*ð*um ; 330. 6, *ð*one *w*elegan ac *ð*one *w*ædlan ; 354. 21, *m*æden and *m*odor ; 406. 3, *s*cea*ð*um to *s*creafe ; 458. 29, *g*ymmum and *g*yrlum ; 470. 18, *w*ur*ð*mynt and *w*uldor ; 490. 12, *g*eswinc and *s*arnyss ; 506. 8, *b*ylde and *b*lisse ; 538. 21,

*b*letsung and *b*eorhtnys ; 576. 31, caseras and cyningas ; 590. 15, *f*earra *f*læse, oððe *b*uccena *b*lod ; 592. 16, *w*op and *w*anung; 606. 22, on *w*orde oððe on *w*eorce ; 610. 27, mid *m*icelre *m*ihte and *m*ægenðrymme.

A. H. II.

20. 33, mid *m*uðe ge mid *m*ode ; 68. 17, corn and ceaf ; 78. 19, ne ðurh *y*lde ac ðurh *y*felnysse ; 140. 19, ðære *d*eofles *d*yderunge ; 194. 30, *l*of mid ge*l*eafan ; 212. 1, *s*yfernysse and *s*oðfæstnysse ; 222. 2, on sumum sea*ð*e *s*weartra *s*ynna ; 222. 29, to *w*udunge and to *w*æterunge ; 270. 22, buton *b*lode and *b*ane ; 276. 19, *l*ichama and *l*eomu ; 306. 11, ma*ð*m on *m*oldan ; 500. 17, *w*ædligum and *w*anscryddum.

W. H.

Wulfstan makes this alliterative combination such a feature of his prose that I have endeavoured to present all the occurrences of manifest alliteration that are to be found in this collection of homilies.

3. 3, *s*teorran and *s*treamas, . . . *f*leotende *f*ixas and *f*leogende *f*ugelas, . . . *w*yrmas and *w*ildeor; 5. 4, *m*ihta, *m*ærða and *m*yrhða, so 35. 2, 144. 27, 153, 20, 167. 8, 281. 11 ; 12. 11, his *b*roces *b*ote secð ; 16. 12, of *d*eofles gewealde and of helle *w*ite ; 33. 15, *l*ara and *l*aga, so 65. 22, 66. 2, 8, 67. 11, 108. 4, 133. 1, 154. 21, 159. 1, 268. 4, 307. 19, 308. 26 ; 37. 16, eallum *m*ode and eallum *m*ægene, so 20. 1, 109. 6, 143. 3, 234. 24, 264. 7 ; 40. 7, *m*ordres oð*ð*on *m*anslihtes, *s*tala ne *s*trudunga ; 40. 9, wið *g*itsunga and *g*ifernessa, so 68. 14 ; 40. 14, ne *w*igelunga ne *w*iccecræfta ; 40. 16, *d*eofles *g*edwimera ; 40. 22, wið *d*eofles *d*are ; 51. 32, ne mid *w*orde ne mid *w*eorce, so 54. 16, 67. 16, 73. 18, 76. 2, 112. 10, 142. 20, 143. 15, 144. 22, 167. 3, 179, 12, 278. 31, 279. 2, 292. 31 ; 53. 10, ongean *m*odstaðolnysse and *m*odes *s*trencðe ; 71. 5, *f*reolsa and *f*æsten, so 113. 1, 164. 9 ; 73. 7, *w*ealdend and *w*yrhta, so 107. 32, 108. 5, 179. 31, 308. 24 ; 73. 16, *s*ibbe and *s*ome, so 112. 12, 118. 3, 272. 22 ; 73. 20, mid *l*eohte and *l*acum ; 74. 7, *d*omas and *d*ihtas ; 74. 8, *l*eod and *l*agu ; 74. 16, on . . . *m*ode and *m*uðe ; 74. 18, on ge*ð*ance and on *ð*eawum ; 82. 14, *b*lis and *b*ot ; 86. 10, *h*ol and *h*ete and *r*ypera *r*eaflac, *h*ere and *h*unger, *b*ryne and *b*lodgyte and *s*tyrnlice

styrunga, stric and *steorfa* ; 91. 14, Godes mihta and his *mildheort-nesse* ; 93. 21, of *dea*ð*e* to *dome* ; 114. 4, *sorgung* and *sargung, so* 209. 16 ; 115. 8, *man* and *mor*ð*or* and *manslihtas, stala* and *stru-dunga* and *searacræftas,*—note that *s* is probably intended to allit-erate with *st,* thus corresponding to the three *m*'s which alliterate in the preceding combination. 115. 10, wið *forliger* and wid *æg-hwylce fyl*ð*e* ; 128. 4, *bersta* and *bismra, so* 157. 1, 268. 13; 129. 1, *here* and *hungor, bryne* and *blodgyte, so* 172. 17, 243. 2, 268. 21 ; 129. 3, *hol* and *hete* and *rypera reaflac, here* and *hunger, bryne* and *blodgyte* and *styrnlice styrunga, stric* and *steorfa, so* 159. 10 ; 129. 17, ð*urh mor*ð*dæda* and ð*urh mandæda,* ð*urh stala* and ð*urh strutunga,* ð*urh gitsunge* and ð*urh gifernessa, so* 163. 21 ; 132. 14, *welan* and *wiste* ; 133. 3, *wædl* and *wawa* . . . *here* and *hunger, so* 159. 8, 169. 16, 268. 22; 133. 7, *stalu* and *steorfu,* 243. 3; 138. 14, ð*earfan* and ð*eodcyningas, earme* and *eadige, so* 138. 15 ; 139. 3, *wop* and *wanung* ; 139. 22, mid *sorge* and mid *sare, so* 139. 26, 153. 23; 140. 1, *wuldor* and *wyr*ð*mynt*; 157. 19, *mæ*ð*e* and *munde, so* 243. 12, 266. 9; 159. 10, *hol* and *hete* ; 159. 11, *rypera reaflac* ; 159. 12, us *unwedera* for oft weoldan *unwæstma* ; 162. 7, ð*egene* and ð*ræle* ; 162. 14, *here* and *hete* ; 164. 2, ð*urh swiedomas* and ð*urh searacræftas* ; 164. 4, ð*urh mægræsas* and ð*urh manslihtas* ; 181. 2, buton *golde* and *glænegum* ; 184. 14, *man* and *mor*ð*or, so* 241. 9 ; 185. 9, fram *wlite* and fram *wuldre* ; 186. 4, se ð*eostra* ð*rosm,* ð*æra lyfta leoma* and ð*æra ligetta blæst* . . . seo *grimme gesyh*ð and seo *godcunde* miht, se *hata* scur and *helwara hream,* ð*æra beorga geberst* and ð*æra bymena* sang, se *brade bryne* ofer eall woruld and se *bitera* dæg, se *micla cwealm* and ð*æra* manna *mân,* seo *sare sorh* and ð*æra sawla gedal,* se *sara* sið and se *sorh-fulla* dæg, ð*æt brade bealo* and se *byrnenda* grund, ð*æt bitere* wite and se *blodiga* stream, *feonda fyrhto* and se *fyrena* ren ; 187. 18, in *mor*ð*re* and on *mane,* in *susle* and on *sare,* in *wean* and on *wyrm-slitum* betweonum *dea*ð*um* and *deoflum,* in *bryne* and on *byter-nesse,* in *bealewe* and on *bradum* ligge, in *yrm*ð*um* and on *earfe*ð*um,* on *swyltewale* and in *sarum sorgum,* in *fyrenum bryne* and on *ful-nesse* ; 190. 2, *halige heapas* symle *wunia*ð on *wlite* and on *wuldre* and on *wynsumnesse* æfre ; 190. 3, ð*ær bi*ð *mær*ð and *myrh*ð ; 198. 2, *wyrhta* and *wealdend ealra worulda* ; 202. 18, se is *yrm*ð*a* dæg and *ealra earfo*ð*a* dæg ; 204. 1, ð*eofan* and ð*eodscea*ð*an* . . .

wiccan and *wigleras*; 204. 4, manslagan and . . . manswican . . .
mansworan and *morðwyrhtan* . . . ryperas and *reaferas*; 230. 1,
eower *word* and eower *wedd*; 232. 23, *scip* and *sceld*; 241. 11,
mid *deoflum* and mid *dracum* and mid *wælslitendum* *wyrmum*;
242. 18, on *wlite* and on *wynne*; 243. 3, *unwæstm* and *unweder*;
243. 6, *rædes* and *rihtes*; 252. 6, to *hæle* and to *helpe*; 257. 11,
mid *wlencum* and mid *wiste*; 257. 12, *swangor* and *swær*; 263. 22,
foldan fægernes; 266. 28, ðeofas and ðeodsceaðan, *ryperas* and *reaferas, leogeras* and *liceteras, wedlogan* and *wærlogan*; 267. 4, *frið*
and *fultum*; 267. 28, for *feo* ne for *freondscipe*; 268. 19, wa heom
ðæs *wærscipes* and ealles ðæs *weorðscipes*; 274. 21, *frið* and *freondscipe*; 274. 24, manslagan and *manswican*; 275. 2, *wordlagan* and
wedlogan; 286. 19, minne *bertun* and minne *berun*; 298. 15,
ryperas and *reaferas*; 307. 12, *bocum* and *gebedum*; 308. 28, mid
leohte and *lacum*; 308. 31, *freolsa* and *fæstena*; 309. 21, wiccean
oððe *wigelearas, horingas* oððe *horewenan, morðwyrhtan* oððe
mansworan; 310. 1, manslagan and *mægslagan* . . . ðeofas and
ðeodsceaðan, *ryperas* and *reaferas, leogeras* and *liceteras* and *leod-
hatan* hetele.

B. H.

11. 2, on *domes dæge*; 11. 31, to *wlitignesse* and to *weorðunge*;
17. 21, *leoht* ðæs ecan *lifes*; 23, 6, swa *wite* swa *wuldor*, so 97. 21;
25. 24, *wræc* and . . . *wite*; 45. 8, mid *lufe* ge mid *laðe*; 53. 9,
to *wean* and to *wlencum*; 57. 36, ðes *blowenda wudu* and das
blowendan wyrta; 61. 36, *sar* and *sace*; 71. 20, doð sceaðum to
scrafum; 83. 22, ðæt *wite* and ðæt ece *wræc*; 83. 32, setunga and
searwa; 97. 33, mid ealle *mod* and *mægene*, so 209. 24; 105. 31,
to *helpe* and to *hæle*; 111. 15, *lufon* and *geleafan*, so 171. 25,
173. 13; 111. 33, *welan* and his *wista*; 113. 16, mid *wlite* and
mid *wæstmum*; 169. 27, *wuldor* and *weorðung*; 173. 8, searwa
and yfel sacunga; 173. 17, to his *healle* and to his *hirede*; 203. 21,
on *fultum* and on *frofre*, so 201. 28, 203. 26.

The rare instances that occur hardly justify the separate group
of (*c*.), the Adjective and the dependent Noun; the following
may, however, be noted as illustrative of the few conventional
forms: W. H., 74. 12, *milde* on *mode*; 79. 7, *wide* on *worulde*;
145. 34, *wise* on *wordum*.

The group, (*d*.) Adjectives and Adverbs in close sequence, draws nearly all its instances from Wulfstan; the instances in Ælfric and B. H. being in some cases mere formulæ.

A. H.

236. 14, calle ðing gelice eaðe, and nan ðing earfoðe; 266. 26, mycele and manega; 292. 12, dumbe and deafe; 478. 14, hreowlice and hrædlice; 490. 15, soð lif and gesælig; 544. 28, mid strecum mode and stiðum life.

W. H.

5. 2, halte wurdan hale; 19. 10, gecorene and gecwene; 40. 4, ne lease ne luðerfulle ne fule ne fracode, so 107. 14; 40. 20, ne færinga to fægene, so 70. 13; 40. 21, to slapole ne ealles to slence; 48. 2, dimne and deopne; 52. 29, wærne and wisne, so 55. 21; 79. 4, swæslice swicole; 91. 12, swytol and gesyne, so 159. 5, 163. 14; 109. 2, lytel is se fyrst ðyses lifes, and lyðre is ðæt we lufjað; 133. 13, sorhful and sarigmod; 138. 7, read and reðe; 145. 16, earmum and eadgum; 145. 23, forsceapene . . . and bescofen; 149. 18, swa mihtig and mare; 154. 4, sarig and sorhful; 162. 22, rancne and ricne; 180. 10, georne and girne; 184. 20, ne ðæs heardes ne ðæs huesces ne ðæs wraðes ne wynsumes ne ðæs eaðes ne ðæs earfoðes ne ðæs leofes ne ðæs laðes; 225. 32, ða deorcan and ða dimman stowe; 247. 21, wær . . . and wis; 273. 5, hu læne and hu lyðre ðis lif is, hu sarlic and hu sorhful and hu geswincful; 273. 10, seoc and samhal; 275. 15, wislice and wærlice; 305. 7, fullic and fracodlic.

B. H.

71. 4, milde and monðwære; 109. 25, neddearf and nytlic; 175. 6, sceama and scyldig; 199. 36, weoroldlice and wislice; 203. 36, swutole and gesyne.

(*e*.) Verbs in close sequence.

A. H.

24. 16, sealde and gesette; 48. 29, fylstendum oððe feohtendum, 50. 18, clypode and cwæð,—very frequent—a translation of the

common Biblical expression. 78. 16, *gewylt* and *gewissað*; 148. 3,
ne ferde heo *worigende* . . . ac wæs *wunigende*; 154. 27, ge *wyexð*
ge *wanað*, so II 214. 32; 268. 31, *mihte* and *moste*; 320. 20, *byr-*
nende . . . and *bodigende*; 356. 27, Criste gedafenað ðæt he *weaxe*
and me ðæt ic *wanigende* beo; 388. 20, *ofylled* and *gefrefrod*;
568. 9, ic gewyllade and ofer*wann*; 606. 20, *tæcende* and *tihtende*.

W. H.

11. 8, *dwelode* . . . and *adwealde*; 19. 7, *gedreht* and *gedrefed*;
39. 11, *bidde* and *beode*, so 120. 1, 8, 246. 19, 291. 2; 40. 7, *gewi-*
tan ne *gewyrhtan*; 46. 8, *wealdan* and *wunjan*; 47. 15, *habban* ne
healdan,—very frequent. 50. 7, *magan* and *motan*,—very frequent.
53. 17, *sæwð* and *sendeð*; 68. 1, *rype* oððe *reafige*, so 163. 12;
68. 6, *weorðjan* and *werjan*, so 143. 20, 179. 26, 309. 1; 70. 8, ne
tyrje ne ne *tyne*, so 309. 4; 73. 11, ne ænig ne *syrwe* ne oðrum ne
swige; 74. 22, *lufjan* and *læran*; 75. 17, *sang* and *sæde*; 86. 19,
gehealden and *geholpen*; 90. 2, *wacigean* and *warnjan*; 90. 17, *segð*
and *swutelað*; 91. 18, *derjað* and ðearle *dryfað*; 100. 4, *clypode*
and *cwæð*, so 141, 4; 101. 9, *gedreeð* and *gedwelað*; 109. 16,
lufjan and . . . *gelyfan*; 122. 1, ðrowian and ðolian, so 151. 30;
130. 6, *forloren* and *forlogen*, so 164. 8; 132. 11, *wissode* and
warnode; 132. 21, *rædan* and . . . *aræran*; 134. 2, *rede* and *ryme*;
137. 23, *amasod* and *amarod*; 138. 7, *byrnð* and *braslað*; 143. 17,
wanað oððe *wyrdeð*, so 143. 21; 143. 21, *fyligean* and . . . *fadjan*;
151. 26, *lærð* and *laðað*, so 241. 26; 154. 17, *laðjað* and *logjað*;
163. 11, *hergjað* and *heawað*; 163. 12, *bændað* and *bisnrjað*;
166. 5, *betan* . . . ðæt we ær *bræcon*; 183. 2, *wepað* and *wanjað*;
185. 6, to *smeagenne* and to *sorgjanne*; 218. 29, *healdan* and
haligan; 229. 27, ic *hate* and ic *halsige*; 236. 8, *lærde* . . . and
lædde, so 242. 12, 275. 15; 262. 15, *geðreade* and *geðræste*;
266. 5, *wenjan* and *weman*; 266. 29, *hatjan* and *hynan*; 267. 20,
stalige . . . and *strangje*; 276. 6, ðurh *larleaste* ne *lædan* ne *læran*
ne *leacnjan*; 309. 2, *frefrjan* and *fedan*; 302. 27, *amette* and *amear-*
code; 303. 22, *manjan* and *mingjan*; 307. 7, *bodjan* ge *bysnjan*, so
307. 13.

B. H.

15. 21, *cleopode* and . . . *cwæð*,—very frequent in B. H., more
so than in the other Homilies. So the following: 71. 10, *cegdon*

and cwædon; 105. 9, sungon and sægdon; 139. 16, cleopigende and cegende. 81. 30, ge*l*yfdon and hine *l*ufodon; 87. 11, *h*opodan and *h*yhtan; 95. 24, *m*agan and *m*otan; 99. 7, gefyllan and gefrætwiað; 103. 12, *w*yscton and *w*ilnodon; 109. 11, mynige and manige, so 161. 1, 197. 2; 111. 17, reccean, and rædan; 113. 31, *l*of *l*eornjan and ðæt *l*æran; 151. 16, forbrecan and forbærnan; 197. 5, to *w*eorðienne and to *w*uldrienne; 199. 2, gewcox and gewriðode; 213. 17, *f*ultmian and . . . *f*refran. Many of these cases are stereotyped.

BOETH.

The instances of alliteration in Boethius are so infrequent that separate grouping is not called for. The most probably intentional instances are as follows: viii. 4, for ðæm *m*ihtlicum and *m*anigfealdum *w*eoruldbisgum; 10. 17, mid *g*olde and mid *g*imme; 40. 28, *w*elig on *w*æstmum; 42. 30, *w*lite and *w*ela; 48. 25, be*h*yd . . . and be*h*elod; 62. 4, on *b*radum *b*rede; 102. 4, *w*eligne oððe *w*ealdendne; 114. 17, *m*onnum and *m*agum; 124. 17, *w*ist and *w*æda; 140. 2, *s*temn and *s*taðol; 140. 10, *w*undorlic and *w*insum; 144. 29, *f*riðstop and . . . *f*rofer; 148. 29, *f*riðað and *f*yrðrað; 150. 13, *w*eaxað and eft *w*aniað; 156. 34, *m*anegum and *m*istlecum; 158. 25, reht and ræt; 166. 13, *m*anega and *m*istlece *b*isna and *b*ispell; 180. 12, *l*ofes oððe *l*eana; 200. 3, *m*icelne *w*ean and *m*anigfealdne *w*ete,—transverse alliteration.   206. 23, cystum and · cræftum; 208. 10, *y*felwillende and *y*felwyrcende; 218. 19, *m*anega and *m*istlice gemettunge; 224. 11, ge*h*yt and ge*h*elt; 226. 22, miscað and metgað; 260. 1, *w*yrhta and *w*ealdend.

Dr. O. Hoffmann[1] has made a study of the "rime-forms" in West-Germanic; he considers first, forms in which both members of the combination are related merely by a similarity of meaning, and second, in which both members are related by a similarity of sound, either initial or final. Though the investigation is made mostly in poetic monuments, attention is also given to the prose. The dialects considered are Old High German, Old Saxon, Frisian, and Anglo-Saxon.

Anglo-Saxon poetry, being alliterative, must greatly favour the production of "rime-forms," and, naturally, the proportion is

---

[1] O. Hoffmann: *Reimformeln in West Germanischen.* Darmstadt, 1885. Diss.

much greater in poetry than in prose. Dr. Hoffmann[1] raises the question whether the presence of so many such forms in the prose, existing beside so many more in the poetry, can be taken as proof of a widespread use in popular speech. It is certain that a writer or speaker, acquainted with the classics of Beowulf, Cynewulf, and the "Cædmon" poems, must have a larger command of these forms than any illiterate person could have. At the same time, those prose works in which they occur most frequently—the Homilies—were addressed to the common people, and would most likely reflect many of the peculiarities of the common speech. We can hardly doubt that usual collocations of the written discourse, as 'clypode and cwæð,' 'dumbe and deaf,' 'sang and sægde,' etc., must have pervaded the colloquial speech as well. We realize the difference between the artistic and the popular use when we compare the figure of the genuine homilies of Wulfstan with the figure of the homilies of Ælfric. Ælfric's " rime-forms " seem to be in many cases popular formulæ and not the result of individual creation ; Wulfstan, we clearly realize, is inventing new and startling forms to give impressiveness to his speech.

In the instances quoted above, the majority of the examples consist of words joined by conjunctions or closely related syntactically. The instances are infrequent where the author connects, like Lyly in his *Euphues*, several sentences by the bond of alliteration. The alliteration was confined to the chief words of the clause or simple sentence, and was, in prose, largely influenced by the frequent joining, in poetry, of alliterating words in the first half of the verse.

Wulfstan alone makes alliteration an artistic element. He realized its rhetorical effectiveness in the delivery of his message to the people, and used it abundantly in those homilies in which his fervour is greatest. Joining it, as he frequently does, with rime, he unites the metrical principles of the old and the new poetry, and, if he does not give us fine prose according to our recognized canons, he at least was the author of prose which must have stirred the minds of his hearers. We shall have to consider this prose further when we deal with *Rime.*

[1] p. 30.

The fact that in neither A. H. nor B. H. is there any use made of alliteration above the ordinary level of the prose, confirms our opinion that it was a recognized property of popular speech. It is much the same as with the tropes. The tropes of the homilies are such as might readily occur in colloquial speech, allowance being made for a more finished form in the written discourse; these alliterative combinations are in such contrast to Wulfstan's and are generally of such a moderate nature that we can hardly deny that they are taken almost directly from the popular speech.

When we turn from the public addresses of the preachers to the literary labour of the translator, we realize the purpose of the figure. Alliteration is intended for the ear, not the eye; and, as the translation of the *Boethius* was not intended for oratorical delivery, the purpose of the figure would not here be served. Only such instances are found as are probably in common use. Thus 'wlite and wela,' 'wist and wæda,' 'reht and ræt,' etc., are among the most usual of the alliterative formulæ.

β. *Rime.*

Rime is very little used in Ælfric, and in the few instances of its occurrence it is doubtful whether it should be considered as an accident or as a rhyming combination not peculiar to any one writer. Such instances as 4. 32, yfelnyss and ðwyrnys, 38. 1, herigendra and singendra, etc., should, perhaps, be regarded as accidental.

The following examples may, however, be considered as more or less intentional :

44. 24, forebcacena and . . . tacna; 66. 9, ætes and wætes, so frequently; 138. 2, hylt and gewylt; 268. 12, hwæðer he aht sy oððe naht.

II 8. 15, growende and blowende, so 8. 18; II 94. 32, dearnunge oððe earnunge; II 208. 9, seðe wyrigð fæder oððe moder oððe hi tyrigð.

The following instances of Grammatical Rime[1] have been noted in Ælfric :

8. 27, ealra hlaforda Hlaford, ealra cyninga Cyning; 14. 23, ban of minum banum and flæsc of minum flæsce; 132. 23, forligras

---

[1] See *P. B. B.*, IX. p. 426; and below, p. 52.

mid forligrum, gitseras mid gitscrum, sceaðan mid sceaðum, ða
forsworenan mid forsworenum ; 168. 3, oferswiðan urne deað
mid his hwilwendlicum deaðe ; 190. 19, ealra witegena witegung ;
190. 34, Crist is soð witega and ealra witegena witega ; 198. 14, he
is soð god of soðum gode ; 258. 31, god of gode ; 286. 8, deadlice
of undeadlicum ; 358. 6, witegan mid heora witegunge ; 410. 21,
yfel ofer yfel and ðwyrnysse ofer ðwyrnysse ; 410. 23, stan ofer
stan ; 490. 2, cildhad gewit to cnihthade ; 494. 30, soð god of
soðum gode, ælmihtig Sunu of ðam Ælmihtigan Fæder.

ɪɪ 14. 22, ealra halgena Halga ; 136. 14, weste on ðam westene ;
274. 27, deaðe ðam ecum deaðe ; 282. 23, fram unðeawum to
godum ðeawum ;' 324. 34, godre gymene to godum ðeawum ;
410. 9, sind gold and seolfor yfele yfelum and gode godum ;
484. 17, yfel mid yfele forgyldað ; 568. 10, gefeoht cymð ofer
gefeohte, gedrefnys ofer gedrefnysse, eorðstyrung ofer eorðstyr-
unge, hungor ofer hungre, ðeod ofer ðeode, and ðonne gyt ne
cymð se brydguma.

W. H.

40. 4, ne to swicole ne to ficole, so 82. 2 ; 56. 8, ðurh deofles
dara and his unlara ; 68. 19, rumheortnys and syfernes, clænnes
and modðwærnes, glædnes and anrædnys, sybgeornes and ead-
modnes, so 68. 14 ; 72. 5, seðe wære gifre, weorðe he syfre ; 72. 6,
seðe wære galsere . . . weorðe se clænsere, so 74. 1 ; 74. 6, werje
man and nerje ; 78. 8, rihtlice and wærlice ; 81. 3, swilce earfoð-
nessa and swilce gedrefednessa ; 81. 15, to wlance and ealles to
rance ; 82. 11, wide and side,—a common phrase. 86. 9, sacu
and clacu, so 106. 26 ; 94. 2, wanung and granung,—frequent.
103. 1, ætes and wætes ; 105. 9, wolice and gedwollice,—the difference in the quantity of the root vowels will hardly exclude this
example. 106. 26, saca and wraca, so 133. 3 ; 114. 4, sorgung and
sargung, so 209. 16 ; 129. 3, stalu and cwalu, so 132. 16, 159. 9,
268. 22 ; 132. 17, bitan aud slitan, so 191. 16 ; 132. 23, blisse and
lisse, so 134. 4, 237. 5, 265. 12 ; 137. 5, dreosað and hreosað ;
139. 19, byrnað and yrnað ; 139. 32, ne lyre ne deaðes gryre ;
143. 9, griðjan and friðjan, so 179. 24, 308. 28 ; 158. 8, berypte
ealra gerihta and innan bestrypte ælcra gerysena ; 164. 3, ðurh
lahbricas and ðurh æswicas ; 191. 15, bewarjan and bewerjan,—

4

not a perfect rime. 245. 2, granjað and wanjað; 253. 5, ne morðor to begangenne ne aðas to swerianne ne niðas to fremmanne ne leasunga to sæcganne ne ðeofenda to begangenne; 259. 22, groweð and bloweð; 309. 20, wite and lahslite.

Grammatical Rime.

47. 26, nuriht to rihte; 154. 2, ealra bisceopa bisceop.

B. H.

5. 32, wordum and dædum; 21. 34, onginneð and ðonne ablinneð; 58. 2, growende and blowende, so 111. 5; 115. 12, forwordenlic and gedrofenlic and gebrosnodlic and feallendlic; 161. 6, witon . . . and ongyton; 161. 7, mærsienne and weorðienne; 165. 30, halette and grette; 185. 7, wop and grop; 247. 33, brædon and . . . cwædon.

Grammatical Rime.

31. 25, se ælmightiga from ðon ælmihtigan and se eca from ðan ecan; 89. 20, hire flæsc of minum flæsce and hire ban of minum banum; 107. 26, ðeod wið ðeode; 223. 32, yfel mid yfele.

Boeth.

82. 10, foremære and widmære; 104. 34, heora eaðmetto . . . heora ofermetta; 130. 6, grewð and blewð; 154. 28, beorhtre and leohtre; 156. 6, rihtwislice and gesceadwislice.

Grammatical Rime.

54. 12, ænig wiðerweard ðing bion gemenged wið oðrum wiðerweardum, so 74. 19; 136. 12, se hehsta god is ælces godes fullast; 182. 9, God ealra goda; 202. 27, dælan ða yfelan ðam yfelum, so 230. 25.

γ. *Assonance.*

Gerber[1] defines Assonance as rime with a difference in the final consonant. The figure is rare in Ælfric and the Blickling Homilies, and may be in some of its occurrences the result of chance.

[1] II 168.

A. H.

4. 34, to ccum forwyrde ... and to ecere myrhðe; 6. 21, læran and tæcan; 6. 25, gecyrre and lybbe; 10. 16, mihtige and wlitige; 102. 33, on gemete and on getele, so 286. 14; 134. 7, on hadum and on namum; 210. 5, gemanode and gelaðode; 408. 25, sibbe and blisse.

II 90. 15, fortrædon and fugelas tobæron; II 406. 16, hine sylfne bysgað and oðrum gebysnað.

W. H.

5. 9, yrmðe ne myrhðe; 11. 15, ælc broc and nan bot; 33. 15, laga and lara,—very frequently found. 48. 7, mægne and mænege; 52. 31, ymbe swicdom ðonne ymbe wisdom; 71. 1, myrtenes æfre ne abite ne blodes ne abyrige,—note also the alliteration. 72. 13, seðe wære slapol, weorðe se ful wacor; 74. 17, on heortan and weorcan; 90. 18, ge on heofonlicum tunglum ge on corðlicum styrungum; 129. 7, fela syn forsworene and swiðe forlogene and wed eac abrocene, so 268. 27; 130. 6, forloren and forlogen, so 164. 8; 132. 21, rædan and swiðe aræran; 137. 23, amasod and amarod; 138. 2, gcypte oððe gecydde; 139. 3, stearc and heard; 147. 17, asecgan and areccan; 151. 6, ðrowjan and doljan, so 151. 30; 151. 11, totwænað and todælað; 157. 13, lytel ne mycel; 159. 8, bryne ne blodgyte; 161. 11, forsworene and swiðe forlogene; 162. 14, here and hete; 164. 10, Godes wiðersacan and cyrichatan; 185. 12, aðystrode and adysgode; 199. 19, oferswyð hy and oferslyhð hy; 200. 3, to bycgenne oððe to syllenne; 203. 13, ðær is ece bryne ... and ðær is ece gryre; 209. 17, ðær is wyrma slite and calra wædla gripe; 235. 15, potedon and ðoddetton; 250. 13, miltse and blisse; 253. 16, ymbhydige and gemyndige; 266. 16, fyrðrje and fryðje; 269. 5, fyrðrige and wurðige; 276. 9, lædan oððe ... læran; 303. 21, ða læwedan and ða ungelæredan; 310. 1, cyrichatan and sacerdbanan.

B. H.

43. 8, tæcan and læran; 55. 5, agifan and agildan; 55. 28, gedwan and gewat; 67. 32, behydig and gemyndig; 171. 27, wið deofla niðum and helle witum; 191. 13, brædon and lærdon; 227. 5,

to hæle and to ræde; 229. 21, beheald nu and geseah; 229. 27, mycel leoht and frea beorht; 243. 9, ðin gilp and ðin hiht.

BOETH.

4. 31, swiðe totorenne and swiðe tobrocenne; 8. 10, scippend and rihtend; 10. 13, ðæt he on heora ðeowdome beon mot, ðonne bið he on ðam hehstan freodome; 92. 27, earmran and eargran; 128. 20, geðohtest and geworhtest; 144. 28, ðam ystum and ðam yðum.

Kluge[1] discusses the history of Rime in Germanic with special reference to Anglo-Saxon. The following forms are discriminated: *Athalhending*, as in 'wordhord'; *Skothending*, as in 'wægnðegn'; combinations like 'ceorl and eorl'; *Grammatical rime*, as in 'lað wið laðum'; *Sectional rime*, as in 'bord ord onfeng'; *Etymological rime*, as in 'dogora dægrim'; *Suffix rime*, as in 'ongan fremman'; and the rime, either *athalhending* or *skothending*, used to connect the two short lines of one long line, or the second short line of one long line with the first short line of the next.

The treatment is, of course, concerned mostly with the poetry, and is of value in this connection as showing the extent to which the device was used. From *Beowulf* to Layamon's *Brut*, there is a more or less steady increase in the use of rime,[2] an increase which cannot be merely the result of chance.

Sievers[3] objects to Kluge's consideration of the suffixal rime as a special artistic form, because it is concerned merely with the similarity of syllables which in verse are unaccented. The objection is, to a certain extent, valid and applies to prose as well as to poetry. There are, nevertheless, instances of this rime quoted above which seem to possess a certain rhetorical value. Thus 'wordum and dædum' must have excited a certain amount of pleasure in the recurrence of the similar sound, even though that sound occurred in the unaccented syllables. The fact that we find further instances of three or more words joined together and all with the same unaccented suffix, would seem to justify us in assuming for the

---

[1] *P. B. B.*, IX. 422.   [3] Paul's *Grundriss der Germ. Phil.*, II. 893.
[2] *loc. cit.*, p. 445.

suffixal rime a certain, though necessarily unimportant, place in the rhetorical economy of the prose structure. In rhetorical effect it cannot compare with rime in the accented syllables; yet it cannot be utterly disregarded.

The function of rime had not yet become established in poetry. It was at the time of Ælfric in the transitional stage on the way to its adoption as a definite device in poetic expression. During this period of its evolution it is but natural that it transgresses the limits of poetry and attempts liberties with the prose structure. Prose was yet far from having attained a perfect standard. It admitted many of the licenses which were the natural right of poetry. Alliteration, we saw, was found to a large extent in the prose of Wulfstan and to a lesser extent in that of Ælfric and the Blickling Homilist. This was a characteristic element in Anglo-Saxon verse; yet the unformed condition of the prose permitted its intrusion. The same is true with reference to rime, except that its presence in prose is less an appropriation of a strictly poetic device than is alliteration. Rime, as remarked above, was not fixed as a distinguishing feature of verse alone.

The above lists of assonance and rime—for all practical purposes they may be considered together—show to what a comparatively large extent these figures occur in the prose. There are instances of rime, as of alliteration, which are not included in these lists, because it was felt that they did not possess rhetorical value; they were merely the result of chance. These instances would be composed of those classes of rime which are in their nature unimportant, such as *Suffixal rime, Etymological rime, Grammatical rime.*

It is to be remarked that the feeling for rime as a characteristic of poetic quality is manifest in its use in prose. Except in cases where the riming forms have been frozen into formulæ, or where there is a suspicion of conscious art, rime, like its frequent concomitant, alliteration, occurs for the most part in passages above the average level of excellence. In other words, it here maintains its poetic quality. Wulfstan, who far surpasses the others in his use of all these phonetic figures, is a fine illustration of this fact. In his most impassioned utterances, he makes constant use of all these figures. The other homilists use it, sometimes to strengthen an antithesis, sometimes merely for the sake of the pleasing repetition of the sound; but they never attain to Wulfstan's vivid expression. The translation of the *Boethius*, not being addressed to the ear, contains very few examples, and these are mostly fossilized forms.

Kluge [1] calls attention to the riming forms in the *Charms* and the *Laws*. Such are: 'toslitan oððe tobitan,' 'unclæne ond un-mæne,' 'ræd ond dæd,' in the *Laws;* 'ne *lond* ne *læsse,*' 'ne ferse ne merse,' 'ne *ruh* ne *rum,*' 'ne londes ne strondes,' etc., in the *Charms.* The formation of such rhymes is a characteristic of early speech, and they appear at an early date in chanted language, as in the *Charms,* or in language with the parallel structure in its simplest form, as in the *Laws.* As Kluge [1] says, these rhymes seem to have been very popular, since they appear frequently in the *Laws;* they are a feature also of the older period of the language, and not, as Jacob Grimm [2] says, restricted to the later. If less numerous, they are still on the same footing with the alliterative forms, as we may see from the *Charms.* [3] The combination of Alliteration and Rime in the same words, or the presence of the two figures existing side by side, is very noticeable in Wulfstan.

2. Word-Figures.

A Word-Figure is the repetition of words in a sentence to heighten the effectiveness of speech. The Figures coming under this general head are grouped according to the relation in form of the repeated words to one another, and according to the position of the repeated words in the sentence. These may be considered as

A. Figures of Repetition with reference to the form of words.

B. Figures of Repetition with reference to the position of words.

A. Rhetorical effect may be produced by the repetition of the same word-stem. If the difference in the words is effected by the case-endings or other inflections, the repetition is called *Polyptoton,* if by derivative forms, *Paregmenon.* [4]

Both these figures abound in the prose works that have been examined. Owing to the space which a list of all the examples

---

[1] *loc. cit.,* p. 424.   [2] *Rechtsalt,* [2] 13.
[3] See quotation above.   [4] Gerber, II. 176.

would necessarily occupy, and the comparative unimportance of the figures in a study of style, I shall not include here the instances collected.

In rhetorical effect Polyptoton is superior to Paregmenon. The reason is not far to seek. Except where one noun differs from another in such a detail as an insignificant prefix like *un*, *ge*, etc., the resemblance in sound and meaning is very often obscured by the derivative elements attached to the common stem, and prevents the pleasure, arising from the recognition of a preceding sound, from being realized. Polyptoton, on the other hand, which is an identical repetition with a difference only in the unaccented inflectional ending, presents no hindrance to the recognition of the preceding sound.

In certain cases our authors use the figure with considerable effect. In the balanced and antithetical structure, attention is drawn by the repetition of a leading word to the main thought of the sentence. It is here that Paregmenon reaches its highest effectiveness, as when one word, being the negative of the other, is contrasted with it. 'Undeadlic,' for example, in A. H. 1 224. 16, 'Ðæt an lif is deadlic, ðæt oðer undeadlic,' brings out the idea to be conveyed more strongly than any other word could have done. So, by the repeated recurrence of a word, an idea is forced upon the minds of the audience—for these figures are most effective in spoken discourse,—as in A. H. 1 238. 24, 'god hyrde wæs Petrus and god wæs Paulus and gode wæron ða apostolas.' In this sentence the position of the repeated word has also much to do with its emphasis. The position of the repeated word, indeed, enters as a factor into the rhetorical value of all these examples; the prominent part of the sentence—generally the first—giving importance to the word repeated in it. Those which are placed in no definite order are, for the most part, weaker than those which are repeated in the same relative position.

It is in Ælfric that these figures are used with best taste. His are not the vain repetitions of the Blickling Homilist; his repetitions are not mere substitutes for pronouns. Ælfric attained a higher degree of excellence in his prose style than any other Anglo-Saxon author; in all the word-figures he shows that he understood many of the possibilities of prose. He avoids the

poetic devices of Alliteration and Rime and adopts the legitimate
prose expedient of Repetition. We shall see in the Figures which
follow how careful he is, moreover, not to run into excess.

The abuses of repetition are obvious. A word or a phrase,
repeated without any rhetorical justification, can only destroy the
harmony of the sentence. The Blickling Homilies are most faulty
in this respect. The author repeats words without, apparently,
any thought to rhetorical effect. The repetition may often be the
result of careless writing, as when a word is repeated which
the author had forgotten he had already used. The repetition is
also due to a desire on the part of the homilist to avoid all possible,
or impossible, obscurities; a pronoun might often take the place
of the repeated word with greater euphony and as perfect clearness.

In the few instances of these figures in the Biblical translations
of the homilies, the original figure is preserved. In A. H. i
300. 8, 'ðu eart eorðe and ðu gewenst to eorðan. Ðu eart dust
and ðu gewenst to duste,' there is an additional Polyptoton added
in the second part of the verse.

The collocation of the noun and its corresponding verbs, both
syntactically and etymologically related, is not uncommon in these
works, and, as we see from such examples like ' wyrhta wyrcð his
weorc,' it can not be said to possess any great rhetorical value.

It is remarkable that nearly all the instances of Polyptoton
and Paregmenon in the *Boethius* are peculiar to the Anglo-Saxon.
Those examples which are found both in the Latin and the
Anglo-Saxon are as a rule better than the others. The Anglo-
Saxon repeats words for the sake of clearness; the Latin is clear
without this repetition. It is the difference between a youthful
and a mature prose. The Anglo-Saxon version has, however,
many good illustrations of the proper use of these figures. In
strengthening his antitheses, the translator uses repetition with
considerable skill. He can compare well with Ælfric.

B. The other figures of repetition are distinguished by their
position in the sentence. They are classified as follows:[1] (1) the
repetition of the same word in immediate sequence; (2) the repetition of the same expression in the significant parts of the sentence,

[1] Gerber, II. 180.

(*a*) at the beginning, (*b*) at the end, (*c*) at the beginning and end, (*d*) at the end of the preceding and beginning of the following sentence; (3) the repetition of the same words in inverse order; (4) the repetition of the same word in no special order.

1. The Repetition of the Same Word in Immediate Sequence.

The name of this repetition is *Epizeuxis*, which the *Century Dictionary* defines as "immediate or almost immediate repetition of a word involving added emphasis." The figure is so rare and of such weak rhetorical import that the several instances are not worth quoting. We might note, however, among others, A. H. I 336. 14, yrnað, yrnað, and undoð ðæs mynstres geat; 462. 8, geswicað, earme, geswicað cowra offrunga.

A. H. II 182. 8, agif me minne sunu, agif me minne sunu.

W. H. 72. 2, ne latjað na, ne latjað, ac ofstlice efstað and to Gode wendað.

B. H. 15. 18, miltsa me, Dauides Sunu, miltsa me. In the *Vulgate*, the versions of Matthew, Mark, and Luke do not repeat these words in immediate sequence. 87. 8, ðu come to us, middangeardes alysend, ðu come to us heofonwara hyht.

2. The Repetition of the Same Expression in the Significant Parts of the Sentence.

a. At the Beginning.

This figure is called *Anaphora*, and is defined by the *Century Dictionary* as "consisting in the repetition of the same word or words at the beginning of two or more succeeding verses, clauses or sentences."

A. H. I.

66. 25, *eala* ðu cniht, ðe . . . ðine sawle forlure; *eala* ðu cniht, ðu *ne cuðest* ðinne Scyppend; ðu *ne cuðest* manna Hælend; ðu *ne cuðest* ðone soðan freond; 114. 18, ne *talige* nan man his yfelan dæda to Gode, ac *talige* ærest to ðam deofle; 148. 1, ne *lufude* heo na estmettas ac *lufude* fætenu; 162. 23, "se weig is swiðe nearu

and sticol, *seðe læt to* heofonan rice; and se is swiðe rum and
smeðe *seðe læt to* helle wite,"—a free translation of *Matth.* vi. 13,
14, where the Anaphora also exists.   168. 5, *he geðafode* ðam
deofle ðæt he his fandode, and *he geðafode* lyðrum mannum ðæt,
etc.; 168. 26, "ne *lifjað* na se man be hlafe anum, ac *lifjað* be
ðam wordum ðe gað of Godes muðe,"—in *Matth.* vi. 4, of which
this is a translation, the Anaphora does not exist.   172. 2, *his
dyrstignys* hine awreah ða into helle; and eac nu *his dyrstignys*
hine geniðerode; 176. 9, *ungewiss* com se deofol to Criste and
ungewiss he eode aweig; 240. 34, ne *flyhð* he na mid lichaman
ac mid mode.   *He flyhð* forðan ðe he geseah unrihtwisnysse and
unwade.   *He flyhð* forðan ðe he is hyra and ne hyrde; 250. 28,
micel mægen is geleafa, and *micel* is se soða hiht; 252. 14, *getimige*
us tela on lichaman, *getimige* us untela; 252. 30, *and ðu nelt
syllan* ðinum bearne ðrowend for æge, *nele eac God* us syllan
orwenysse for hihte.   *And ðu nelt* ðinum bearne syllan stan for
hlafe, *nele eac God* us syllan heardheortnysse for soðre lufe;
270. 9, *God* lufað us, and *deofol* us hatað.   *God* us fett and
gefrefrað, and *deofol* us wile ofslean; 272. 32, *hraðe* lið ðæt
heofod adune gif ða fet hit ne feriað; and *hraðe* ealle ða lima
togædere forweorðað, gif, etc.; 276. 27, *Ælmihtig God* is se
Fæder, *Ælmihtig God* is se Sunu, *Ælmihtig God* is se Halga
Gast; 278. 6, *æfre* wæs se Fæder and *æfre* wæs se Sunu and *æfre*
wæs se Halga Gast an Ælmihtig God, so 280. 29; 286. 10, *he is
butan* gemete, *forðy ðe he is* æghwær.   *He is butan* getele, *forðon
ðe he is* æfre,—note the assonance in the nouns.   302. 19, *him is
gemæne* mid stanum . . .; *him is gemæne* mid treowum; 336. 29,
ðæt *ðæt ge doð* ðearfum on minum naman, ðæt *ge doð* me sylfum;
482. 16, *ne swera* ðu ðurf heofenan, forðan . . . *Ne swera* ðu
ðurh corðan, forðan . . . *Ne swera* ðu ðurh ðin agen heafod,
forðan . . .,—in the original, *Matth.* v. 34, the word translated *swera* occurs only once.   550. 28, na *beoð ða eadige*, ðe for
hyndum . . . heofiað; ac *ða beoð eadige*, ðe heora synna bewepað;
560. 33, *efne her is* ure hyrde, *efne her is* se frefrigend, so 562. 18.

A. H. II.

34. 6, *mid flæsce* of deaðe aras, and *mid flæsce* to heofonum
astah; 202. 16, *on ðam fifteogoðan dæge* . . . wæs seo ealde æ

geset
204. .
ðæt i
hwiltic
ðode a.
376. 27,
englas .
ðu *lufast*
ðu *lufast* ⟨
wæs ær M⟨
tima stent g
ðisum wordu
him gebeorsci⟩.
wurðran gereorc
frecednysse . . .
mihte.

2. 1, *we* ða *geascodon* b⟨
codon his geceasterwaran b⟨
ðæra engla geferan beon ða g⟨
swutele byscne : *we gesawon* . . . ⟩.
52. 13, *godes* gyfa ne gymað ne g⟨
healdað, so 58. 13, 73. 14, 158. 2 ; ⟨
ðe wislice leofað ; *and se hæfð* andgit, ⟨ ⟩.
and se hæfð godne ræd, ðe him geredað ⟨
modes strengðe, ðe micel mæg forberan . .
ingehyd, ðe godnysse lufað . . . *Se hæfð* ar
bið him sylf, so 59. 6, 69. 13 ; 105. 18, and ⟨
eac on fyr for his færlicum bryne ; *sume* eac on w⟨
hy gelyfdon on ða *eorðan* ; 114. 12, *ðyder sculan* ma
ðider sculan mansworan, *ðyder sculan* æwbrecan . . ., ðy⟨
wiccan . . ., *ðider sculan* ðeofas . . ., so 173. 17, 264. 16, ⟨
121. 11, *ðurh clæne mæden* Crist wearð geboren, and *ðurh*
fulluht we syndon cristene geworden, so 151. 1 ; 123. 18, *ana* ⟨
he . . . deað ðrowode, *and hu he of* deaðe aras, *and hu he*
heofonum astah, *and hu he* ðanan eft . . . to ðam miclum dom⟨
cymð ; 141. 4, *stingað* stranglic sar on his eagan . . . *Stingað*

licum

wela ?

vyðost

e . . . :

ɔ bryne

it ðonne

. *hit færð*

færð suð

ene. And

o for eight

ame phrase.

hine ne mæg

oðerne lædan,

288. 15, *ic wæs*

ɔsthusum ; *ic wæs*

rumod, and ge me

ɔe comon to me,—the

che same Anaphora.

.

reca, and *mycel* ærende brohte he ;
on binne asetene . . . *Weorðian* we
. *Weorðian* we Sancta Marian ; 21. 10,
.en ðyses lænan welan . . . ac *biddan* we
, 33. 25, *hu mycel* Godes geðyld is and *hu*
is,—note the additional Paregmenon. 33. 33,
ðy hine dorste deofol costnian, swylce *he wæs soð*
ɔnglas ðegnedon ; 43. 10, *ne for* rices mannes ege,
, *ne for* nanes mannes lufon ; 89. 21, *ara me* nu, min
for hire wuldres weorðmyndum, *ara me*, ungesæligost
ıfa ; 91. 20, *on ðæm dæge* gewiteð heofon and eorðe . . .
n *ðæm dæge* heofon bið befealden swa swa boc, etc., with
e successive clauses beginning with the same phrase. 93. 30,
ɔdige *syndon* ða men ða ðe wæron unberende, and *eadige syndon*
ða innoðas ða ðe næfre ne cyndon,—the Anaphora is not in the
original, *Matth.* xxiv. 19 ; cf. 159. 28. 99. 23, ac *hwyder gewiton*
ða welan and ða glengas and ða idlan blissa ? oððe *hwyder gewiton*

ða mycclan weorod? so 99. 26; 115. 3, Ꝺeos *woruld* is eall forwordenlic . . . and Ꝺeos *woruld* is eall gewiten; 115. 15, *nu is
æghwonon* hream and wop, *nu is* heaf *æghwonon*, . . . *nu is
æghwonon* yfel and slege; 125. 2, ah *wuton* we ðæt nu geornlice
gemunan . . .; *uton* betan ða geworhtan synna . . .; and *uton*
we symle ðæs dæges fyrhto and egsan on ure mod settan; *uton*
gemunan hu uncuð, etc.; 143. 27, *ic ðe bletsige*, min Drihten, ðu
ðe waldest ealre bletsunge, and *ic bletsige* eal ðin gehat; 145. 12,
we bletsiað ðinne naman mid urum saulum and *we biddað* ðæt ðu
fram us ne gewite; and *we bletsiað* ðe and *we biddað* ðæt ðu
onlyhte ure world; 147. 34, *wes ðu gemyndig* . . . forðon ic beo
ðin hondgeweorc, and *wes ðu gemyndig*, forðon ic healde ðinra
beboda goldhord; 213. 32, ða *sæt* ðær sum ðearfa æt ðæm burg-
geate, *sæt* eac nacod.

Boeth.

22. 17, *hu mihtest ðu* sittan on middum gemænum rice . . .
Hu mihtest ðu beon on midre ðisse hwearfunga? The Latin has
several clauses beginning with *quid si* in II ii. 40, which may
have suggested this figure, but they do not correspond to the
A. S. 50. 24, *for his cræftum* he beoð god if he god beoð, and
for his cræftum he bið anwealdes weorðe gif he his weorðe bið;
132. 28, *ðu eart* sio birhtu ðæs soðan leohtes and *ðu eart* seo
sefte ræst . . .; *ðu eart* ealra ðinga fruma . . .; *ðu eart* . . .
weg; 198. 20, *ic ne sprece* nu no to dysegum monnum, ac *sprece*
to ðam ðe wilniað; 208. 26, *ðingiað* ðæm ðe ðær man yflað and
ne *ðingiað* ðam ðe yfel doð; 258. 1, *ne secð he nanwuht* ne ne
smeað, forðam ðe he hit wat eall; *ne secð he nanwuht* forðæm
he nan wuht ne forleas; 258. 5, *simle he bið* gifende and ne
wanað hys næfre nauht. *Simle bið* ælmihtig . . . *Simle he bið*
lociende . . . *Simle he bið* gelice manðwære. *Simle he bið* ece . . .
Simle he bið freoh.

These instances, which, it will be noticed, are not all pure
Anaphora, comprise those which may be grouped under this figure.
There are many cases in which the repetition occurs near the
beginning of successive clauses or sentences, in the beginning of one
clause and further on in the clause following, or in some other

position; these, with, however, some exceptions, I have not felt
justified in considering as Anaphora.   From the presence of these
irregular repetitions, and the comparative infrequence of true Anaphora—for, when we consider the bulk of the works examined, the
number of examples is not great—we are conscious that Anglo-
Saxon prose writers did not greatly respect those conditions of
position which would have made their repetitions more effective.
The Anaphora of Ælfric and Wulfstan shows that these authors
were not without an appreciation of the rhetorical value of this
figure; in fact, there are many cases in which they made such
use of it as to give real force to their thoughts.   So they
strengthened the Anaphora by the further rhetorical devices of
inversion and transposition.   When the repeated word is carried
out of its usual order to the beginning of the sentence or clause,
emphasis is given by this inversion, which is, of course, increased
by the recurrence of the word in the corresponding position in
the sentence or clause following.[1]

The Blickling Homilist is in this respect also weaker than
the others; he has not, on the whole, the vigour of Wulfstan
nor the polish of Ælfric.   At the same time, he does not fall
into the excess which sometimes marks Wulfstan's work.   The
latter, for instance, in the passage beginning 69. 13, has twenty-
four successive sentences all beginning with nearly the same
words, and in several other places—57. 12, 114. 12, 230. 14,
265. 6—there are five or more clauses with the same beginning.

Seldom, however, as the examples of this figure are in the
homiletic literature we have examined, they are much more
infrequent and much less effective in *Boethius*.   The oratorical

---

[1] That the Homilists knew the rhetorical virtue of a change from the normal
order of words in the sentence, is manifest from the investigations made by
Professor C. A. Smith in his dissertation, *The Order of Words in Anglo-Saxon
Prose*, Baltimore, 1893. The third and fourth chapters deal with Inversion
and Transposition in Alfred's *Orosius* and Ælfric's *Homilies*, and they show
that Ælfric used these devices for rhetorical purposes to about the same extent
as appears in the instances of Anaphora quoted above. Thus of 314 simple
tenses taken from the *Homilies*, "155 are transposed, 139 follow normal order,
while 20 show a mingling;" of the 186 compound tenses, "69 assume normal
order, 53 show complete transposition, while 64 show a mingling of the two."
(p. 26.)

occasion does not exist here; and, as was noticed in considering
the other figures which appeal to the ear, such special devices are
comparatively rare. It will be noticed that in only one instance
is there any suggestion in the Latin which would account for
the presence of the figure in the Anglo-Saxon. An independent
examination of the Latin text of the *Boethius* will show, moreover, that the figure is here rather unusual and of no very great
rhetorical significance; thus '*Nil* periuria, *nil* nocet ipsis Fraus
mendaci compta colore,' is one of the few examples of the figure
to be found in the First Book and rhetorically it is among the best.
The real power of the figure we may learn from the following quotation from Cicero : '*nihilne* te nocturnum præsidium Palatii, *nihil*
urbis vigiliæ, *nihil* timor populi, *nihil* consensus bonorum omnium,
nihil hic munitissimus habendi senatus locus, *nihil* horum ora vult-
usque moverunt.'[1] To say that examples of such power are
not found in Anglo-Saxon is but to say that Anglo-Saxon prose
literature has not the strength of Cicero's orations—for figures
are a measure of literary excellence; and this no one would
venture to deny. That a certain vigorous use, however, is made
of the figure—and in this the Anglo-Saxon of the homilies and
even of this translation surpasses the Latin of the *Boethius*—is
very evident from the examples quoted.

b. At the End.

This figure is called *Epiphora*, and is defined in the *Century
Dictionary* as a " figure in which several successive clauses or
sentences end with the same word or affirmation."

A. H.

18. 9, ðæt wif . . . genam of ðæs treowes wæstm, and *geæt*,
and scalde hire were, and he *geæt;* 140. 28, na for his *neode*,
ac for mancynnes *neode;* 176. 17, ðurh gyfernysse *he wæs oferswiðed* . . .; Ðurh idel wundor *he wæs oferswiðed* . . . Mid
gytsunge *he wæs oferswiðed* . . ., so 198. 33; 212. 3, seðe ne bið
Godes *tempel*, he bið deofles *tempel;* 212. 27, ac his cristendom

---

[1] *Cat.*, I, 2, 1; quoted by Gerber, II, 187.

nis na *herigendlic.* Ac ꝺæs mannes cristendom is *herigendlic;*
248. 7, se Ælmihtiga Fæder is *God,* and his Sunu is Ælmihtig
God; na ꝺry Godas, ac hi ealle an Ælmihtig *God* untodæledlic;
256. 32, ꝺam spedigum *gedafenaꝺ* ꝺæt . . .; ꝺam wædlan *gedafenaꝺ* ꝺæt . . .; 260. 31, nanum ne *gebeode,* ꝺæt ꝺæt he nelle
ꝺæt man him *gebeode;* 262. 14, ꝺæt se synfulla is eorꝺe *gehaten*
and se rihtwisa is heofon *gehaten,* so 278. 21,—the last three
examples quoted are hardly more than grammatical repetitions.
282. 5, ꝺæt ꝺu wylt, ꝺæt ꝺu *lufast;* and ꝺæt ꝺæt ꝺu nelt, ꝺæt
ꝺu ne *lufast;* 282. 27, se Fæder is soꝺ *lufu,* and se Sunu is
soꝺ *lufu,* and se Halga Gast is soꝺ *lufu;* and hi ealle ætgædere an
God and an soꝺ *lufu,* so 282. 29, 284. 8; 284. 6, swa hwæt swa
læsse biꝺ ꝺonne *God,* ꝺæt ne biꝺ na *God,* so 284. 7; 460. 27, on
ꝺam maran ꝺe swiꝺor *syngaꝺ,* and on ꝺam læssan ꝺe hwonlicor
syngaꝺ; 480. 8, gyf ꝺu sylf wille nyꝺer astigan to hellwarum *for
manna alysednysse,* swa swa ꝺu woldest acenned beon *for manna
alysednysse;* 484. 17, seꝺe deraꝺ, derige *gyt swiꝺor;* and se ꝺe
on fulnyssum wunaꝺ, befyle hine *gyt swiꝺor;* 550. 1, Godes
ege is wisdomes *angynn,* and modignys is ælcere synne *anginn;*
592. 10, gif ænig oga is *to ondrædenne,* ꝺonne is se *to ondrædenne;*
594. 6, ꝺu deaꝺes bearn, *gehyr me,* and ꝺu ceaf . . ., *gehyr me.*

A. H. ii.

10. 18, beoꝺ acennede ꝺa geongan mid *mægꝺhade,* and ꝺa
yldran wuniaꝺ on *mægꝺhade;* 22. 15, se mæsta dæl ꝺara manna
ꝺe Gode *geꝺeoꝺ,* ꝺurh clænnysse hi *geꝺeoꝺ;* 68. 17, 'agildan
ꝺam casere ꝺæt him *gebyreꝺ,* and Gode ꝺæt him *gebyreꝺ,*'—in
this free rendering of *Matth.* xxii, 21, the Epiphora is more
marked than in the original. 86. 16, 'Deaꝺes geomerunga *me
becodon,* and helle sarnysse *me becodon,*'—the Epiphora is not
in the original—*Ps.* cxvi, 3. 102. 7, witodlice ꝺam biꝺ dom
buton mildheortnysse, seꝺe nu oꝺrum demꝺ *buton mildheortnysse;*
288. 20, sume teolunga sind ꝺe man *began mæg buton synnum,*
sume sind ꝺe man earfoꝺlice mæg oꝺꝺe nateshwon *buton synnum
began;* 302. 5, fram eastdæle *stemn,* fram westdæle *stemn,* fram
feower windum *stemn;* 312. 30, an is seo ꝺe wæs butan *æ;* oꝺer
is seo ꝺe wæs under *æ;* 344. 1, far . . . na for *woruldlicum*

gestreonum, ne beo ðu carful ymbe *woruldlicum gestreonum;* 368. 26, hi ðry sind on God *untodæledlic,* swa is eac heora hyrdræden *untodæledlic;* 418. 21, swa swa ðu ær wære deofles *bearn,* him *geefenlæcende,* swa ðu bist nu Godes *bearn,* Gode *geefenlæcende;* 440. 26, forðon ðe hit ne bið næfre *ætbroden.* Witodlice ðæt ðæt Martha geceas is hire nu *ætbroden;* 462. 5, seðe is ðæra æhta *hlaford,* he dælð hi swa swa *hlaford;* 524. 3, ege is *twyfeald* and ðeowdom is *twyfeald.* An ege is butan *lufe,* oðer is mid *lufe,* so 524. 5; 572. 9, nu is mildheortnysse *tima,* and ðonne bið domes *tima;* 574. 3, ne cann Drihten *leahtras,* ac hi gewitnað *leahtras;* 574. 6, nat nan man ðyssere worulde *geendunge,* ne furðon his agene *geendunge;* 604. 34, ælc heora is *Ælmihtig God,* ac na swaðeah ðry Godas, ac hi ðry .sind an *Ælmihtig God.*

W. H.

37. 20, ðæt æni cristen man oðrum ne *beode,* buton ðæt he wille ðæt man him *beode,* so 73. 10, 112. 4; 67. 19, ælc ðæra bið Godes *feond,* ðe bið Godes cyrcena *feond,* so 119. 16; 185. 19, se is yrmða *dæg* and calra earfoða *dæg,* so 230. 11; 192. 10, Antecrist bið soðlice *deofol* and *man.* Se sylfa deofol . . . bið soðlice ægðer ge *deofol* ge *man;* 222. 17, ic feola geðrowade *for iow,* ic wæs an rode ahangene *for iow,* and ic dead geðrowade *for iow,* and ic of deaðe aras *for iow;* 224. 9, in Cristes *naman* and in ðære halgan ðrinnesse *naman* and in ðare halgan Anesse *naman* and in ðare halgan rode *naman;* 238. 20, ða soðfæstan men ðonne geseoð heora wuldor . . . *him toweard,* and ða arleasan ðonne gescoð heora wite . . . *him toweard;* 244. 14, oððæt se eahtoða *dæg* cymð; ðæt is domes *dæg,* ðæt is se eca *dæg,* se langa *dæg* æfter ðam dome, se myriga *dæg,* se halgesta sunnan-*dæg,* Godes *dæg,* and calra halgena *dæg;* 266. 22, fylste ðam ðe riht *willan,* and a hetelice styre ðam ðe ðwyres *willan;* 271. 31, ymbe fryðes *bote* and ymbe feos *bote;* 293. 5, se dæg wæs se forma *dæg,* ðe se soða Scyppend . . . *gesceop,* ða ða he ealle ðing *gesceop.*

B. H.

3. 6, Maria cende . . . Crist *on hire innoðe;* Eva cende tearas *on hire innoðe,* so 7. 29; 21. 18, hu mæg ic secan ðæt gastlice

leoht, ðe ic *geseon ne mæg*, oððe hwanon sceol me cuð beon ðæt ic
mid lichomlicum eagum *geseon ne mæg;* 147. 25, heo lufode ma
ðeostro for *hire synnum*, and heo wæs a ðeh gehealden fram *hire
synnum;* 151. 17, ða wæs he gongende to ðære bære, and ða on
middan ðæm lichoman on ðære bære, ða wearð he gefæstnod . . .
to ðære bære; 229. 6, hi hlaf ne æton ne wæter ne *druncon*, ac
æton manna lichoman and heora blod *druncon;* 237. 31, ic bæd
urne Drihtne ðæt he hine *æteowde*, and hraðe he me hine *æteowde;*
239. 27, ðin carcern open we *gemetton*, and ingangende nænige we
ðær *gemetton.*—None of these examples have any special rhetorical
emphasis.

Boeth.

46. 6, hi nellað witan hwæt *hi sint* oððe hwonan *hi sint;*
46. 11, gif hwa nu bið mid hwelcum welum *geweorðod* . . .
hu ne belimpað se weorðscipe ðonne to ðam ðe hine *geweorðod;*
64. 26, forðon ðe on ælcum lande ne *licað* ðæt on oðrum *licað;*
70. 31, mon scyle wenan ðæt heo seo *sio soðe gesælð*, ac sio
wiðerwearde is *seo soðe gesælð;* 72. 31, ge ða ðe *cunnon* ge ða
ðe ne *cunnon;* 80. 23, swa swa ealle wæteru *cumað* of ðære sæ,
and eft ealle *cumað* to ðære sæ; 92. 30, sam hi *dyrfon* sam hi
ne *durfon;* 104. 5, oððe eft se ðe ægðer *ondræt* ge ðone ðe hine
ondræt ge ðone ðe hine na ne *ondræt;* 118. 32, genog ic ðe hæbbe
nu gereht ymbe ða *anlicnessa* . . . ðære soðan *gesælðe.* Ac gif
ðu nu sweotole gecnawan miht ða *anlicnessa* ðære soðan *gesælðe;*
128. 34, eorðan gecynd and wæteres is *ceald*, sie corð is dryge
and *ceald*, and ðæt wæter *wæt* and *ceald;* sie lyft ðonne is
genemned ðæt hio is ægðer ge *ceald* ge *wæt;* 156. 26, ðæt ðu
ne mihte witan hnmeta *he his weolde* oððe hu *he his weolde;*
156. 31, ne me geot nauht ne *tweoð*, ne nu næfre ne *tweoð;*
184. 19, ða wisan ane magon don to gode *ðæt hi wilniað*, ða
yfelan magon onginnon *ðæt hi wilniað;* 190. 28, gif eac hwylc
god man *from gode gewite*, ðonne ne bið he ðe ma fullice god
gif he eallunga *from gode gewite;* 200. 29, ðæs mæstan yfeles
on *ðisse worulde* and ðæs wyrstan edleanes æfter *ðisse worulde;*
212. 11, sio soðe gesælð stent on godra *manna ge earmunga*, and
sio unsælð stent on yfelra *monna ge earmunga;* 214. 12, rihtlice
sceop eall ðæt he *sceop*, so 218. 17, 232. 12 ; 234. 20, gehyt

ðonne *he wyle* and eowað ðonne *he wile* and nimð ðonne *he wile;*
240. 29, forðy hit ne bið *weas gebyred;* ac ðær hit of nauhte ne
come ðonne wære hit *weas gebyred;* 250. 1, ne ðearf hit no eall
geweorðan unawendendlice. Ac sum hit sceal *geweorðan unawendendlice;* 252. 17, he on oðrum ongit *synderlice.* He hine ongit
ðurh eagan *synderlice,* ðurh ða earan *synderlice,* &c.,—repeated
in two more phrases.

The end shares with the beginning the place of emphasis in
the sentence; and Epiphora and Anaphora are the two figures
which gain their force from the fact that the words are repeated
in these respective positions. These figures are more frequent
than the others of identical repetition and possess, on the whole,
more rhetorical vigour. At the same time, we notice that the
figure varies considerably—passing from the hardly more than
grammatical repetition of such a sentence as B. H. 151. 17, 'ða
wæs he gongende *to ðære bære* and ða on middan ðæm lichoman
on ðære bære, ða wearð he gefæstnod be ðære swiðran hand *to
ðære bære,*' which is clumsy and heavy, to the forcible repetitions
of some of the other instances quoted above. The repetitions with
little rhetorical value exist in greater proportion in the *Boethius*
and the *Blickling Homilies;* in the Latin of the former the figure
is very infrequently found. The Blickling Homilist does not seem
to know the possibilities of the figure, for his repetitions betray a
poverty of expression and rarely enforce his ideas. Wulfstan's few
examples are not especially strong, but, for the most part, they are
more than merely grammatical. Ælfric, however, surpasses all
the others in his treatment of the figure, and shows by his instances
of Epiphora that he can command the language to serve his purposes. He makes use, it is true, of the grammatical figure, but he
also attains fine effects with the rhetorical figure.

c. At the Beginning and End.

1. The figure of *Symploce*[1] combines Anaphora and Epiphora.
The *Century Dictionary* defines it as "the repetition of one word
at the beginning and another at the end of successive clauses."

[1] Gerber, II, 193.

The examples are rare in Anglo-Saxon prose, and many of those included in the lists below do not strictly conform to the type.

A. H. I AND II.

12. 19, *God gesceop* to maran engle ðone ðe nu is *deofol;* ac *God* ne *gesceop* hine na to *deofle;* 132. 10, ða yttran ðeostru sind ðæs lichaman blindnyssa wiðutan. Ða inran ðeostru sind ðæs modes *blindnyssa* wiðinnan; 158. 26, *uton biddan leoht* æt urum Drihtne! na ðæt *leoht* ðe *bið geendod* . . .; ac *uton biddan ðæs leohtes* ðe we magon mid englum anum geseon, ðæt ðe næfre ne *bið geendod;* 194. 10, Maria wæs *mæden* ær ðære cenninge and *mæden* on ðære cenninge and *mæden* æfter ðære cenninge, so 546. 8, II 10. 2; 552. 32, *seo ehtnys* him ne becymð to nanre *eadignysse;* ac *seo ehtnys* ana, ðe bið for rihtwisnysse geðolod, *becymð* to ecere *eadignysse.*

W. H.

277. 20, ðæt æfre *ænig ne wearð* ær ðam eorðlic man wisra ðonne *he wearð, ne ænig* eorðlic cyning mærra and mihtigra ðonne *he wearð.*

No examples have been found in the B. H. or *Boeth.* The quotations from A. H. and W. H. show how insignificant the figure is in A. S. prose. It hardly deserves separate treatment.

2. If the same word is repeated at the beginning and end of the same clause or sentence the figure is called *Cyclos.*[1] Another name for the figure is *Epanadiplosis,* which the *Century Dictionary* defines as " a figure by which a sentence begins and ends with the same word."

A. H. I. AND II.

40. 21, *Crist* wunað on godcundnysse and menniscnysse on anum hade an *Crist;* 276. 31, se *Fæder* bið æfre *Fæder,* and se *Sunu* bið æfre *Sunu,* and se *Halig Gast* bið æfre *Halig Gast,* so 280. 27, II 606. 24; 480. 7, *Geswutela* me, gyf ðu sylf wylle nyðer-astigan to hellwarum for manna alysednesse, swa swa ðu

---

[1] Gerber, II, 194.

woldest acenned beon for manna alysednysse; oð̄e gif ic sccole
cyð̄an ð̄inne to-cyme hellwarum . . . *geswutela.*—Note also the
Epiphora in the repetition of 'alysednysse.' II. 36. 4, *getimige*
ð̄am oð̄rum swa him *getimige.*

*d. At the End of the Preceding and Beginning of the Following
Sentence.*

The name of this figure is *Anadiplosis.* It is defined in De
Mille's *Rhetoric*[1] as "that figure by which the word at the end
of one sentence or clause is repeated at the beginning of another."
Only the following instances from *Boethius* are worth noticing:
36. 12, swa swa sigende sond ð̄onne ren *swylgð̄* swa *swylgð̄*
sco gitsung ð̄a dreosendan welan; 42. 26, gif ð̄u nu ð̄æs *gilpst,*
hu ne *gilpst* ð̄u ð̄onne heora godes; 106. 8, ð̄a friend cumað̄
mid ð̄am welan and eft *mid ð̄am welan* gewitað̄; 110. 27, sco
oferfyll simle fet *unð̄eawas* and ð̄a *unð̄eawas* habbað̄ oferð̄earfe
hreowsunga; 122. 18, ð̄onne beoð̄ hit eall *an ð̄ing* and ð̄æt *an
ð̄ing* bið̄ God; 158. 13, ð̄ætte genyht wære *gesælð̄a* and ð̄a
gesælð̄a wæron God,—the Latin has a repetition, but it is not
a case of Anadiplosis,—nonne in *beatitudine* sufficientiam numer-
avimus deumque *beatitudinem* ipsam esse consensimus (III xii.
28). 220. 20, ealle ð̄a ð̄ing ð̄e hire *underð̄ied sint, sint underð̄ied*
ð̄am godcundan foreð̄once; 222. 14, swa doð̄ ð̄a mæstan men on
ð̄am *midmestum* and ð̄a *midmestan* on ð̄am *betstan* and ð̄a *betstan*
on Gode,—note that the cases of the repeated words are different,
and, as in the following instance, the sentence is complete if the
suppressed verb be understood. 254. 1, ne ð̄a styriendan ofer
ð̄a *men* ne ð̄a *men* ofer ð̄a *englas* ne ð̄a *englas* wið̄ God.

3. Repetition of the Same Words in Inverse Order.

"Rhetorical effect is attained if the same words, by external
arrangement or by changed position, direct attention to the ideas
which they represent."[2] One of the figures under this head is
Antimetabole, which the *Century Dictionary* defines as "a rhetorical

---

[1] James De Mille: *The Elements of Rhetoric;* New York, 1878. p. 177.
[2] Gerber, II, 212.

figure in which the same words or ideas are repeated in inverse order."

A. H.

70. 29, gif ðonne eower *Godes miht* ða halgan cyrcan *towurpan* ne mæg, ic *towurpe* eower tempel ðurh ðæs Ælmihtigan *Godes mihte;* 110. 14, nis se man for *steorrum gesceapen,* ac ða ða *steorran* sint mannum . . . *gesceapene,*—Compare *Mark* ii, 27; 130. 31, *hi awurpon* Crist and he *awyrpð hi;* 242. 26, ic *lufige hi* and *hi lufiað* me; 320. 35, ne bið seo *bilewitnys* Gode gecweme butan *snoternysse,* ne seo *snoternys* butan *bilewitnysse,* so 322. 3; Crist *underfeng menniscnysse* on his tocyme, and *men underfengon* God; 256. 31, se *welega* is geworht for ðan *ðearfan* and se *ðearfa* for ðan *welegan;* 274. 7, ealswa we *behofað* ðæt *heofod* ðæra oðera *lima,* swa swa ða *lima behofiað* ðæs *heafdes;* 276. 21, ælc edwist ðætte God *nys,* ðæt is *gesceaft,* and ðæt ðe *gesceaft nys,* ðæt is *God;* 278. 27, *Fyr* acenð of him *beorhtnysse* and seo *beorhtnys* is efeneald ðam *fyre,* so 278. 29; 438. 26, nis on nanum oðrum men *mægðhad,* gif ðær bið *wæstmbærnys;* ne *wæstmbærnys* gif ðær bið ansund *mægðhad;* 578. 7, se *casere* . . . gecneowige æt ðæs *fisceres gemynde,* ðonne se *fiscere* gecneowige æt ðæs *caseres gemynde.*

A. H. II.

46. 7, gemetegie ðæt *fyr* ða *bilewitnysse* ðæt heo to sleac ne sy; and eft getemprie seo *bilewitnys* ðæt *fyr;* 226. 14, seðe *fram Gode* is, he *gehyrð* Godes word; forði ge nellað *gehyran,* forðan ðe ge ne sind *fram Gode;* 234. 6, he *wuldrað* his *Fæder* and se *Fæder wuldrað hine;* 278. 9, ðæt *Crist* beo mid *us,* and *we* mid *Criste;* ðæt *heafod* mid ðam *leomum* and ða *leomu* mid ðam *heafde;* 324. 24, lærde manna *bearn* ðæt hi gebyrsum beon heora *fæderum* a: and ðam *fæderum* bebead, ðæt hi heora *bearn* ne geæbiligdon; 350. 10, ða scuton hwiltidum of ðam weallendum *fyre* into ðam anðræcum *cyle* and eft of ðam *cyle* into ðam *fyre;* 362. 29, nis swaðeah *Fæder* seðe *Sunu,* ne se *Sunu* seðe *Fæder* is; 386. 12, se *mannes Sunu* is *Godes Sunu* and se *Godes Sunu* is *mannes Sunu;* 440. 10, nis ðæt *an ðing* fram *manegum,* ac *manega ðing* sind fram ðam *anum;* 446. 32, seo *sunne* ymbscineð ðone *blindan* and se *blinda* ne gesihð ðære *sunnan* leoman; 448. 1,

God geseah ðone *deofol* and *se deofol* swaðeah wæs bedæled *Godes gesihðe*; 488. 30, to gecigenne mancynn *fram deaðe to life,* na to scufenne *fram life to deaðe;* 586. 28, *he is wisdom* and eal *wisdom is of him.*

W. H.

74. 22, hyran ða *gingran* georne heora *yldran* and lufjan and læran ða *yldran* heora *gingran;* 86. 5, ne byrhð ðonne broðor oðrum hwilan ne *fæder* his *bearne* ne *bearn* his agenum *fæder,* so 128. 10, 149. 28, 159. 16; 168. 11, man oft *herede,* ðæt man sceolde *hyrwan,* and to forð *hyrwde,* ðæt man sceolde *herigean;* 203. 26, swa wendað *wrang* to *rihte* and *riht* to *wrange,* so 228. 23, 297. 28, 298. 20.

BOETH.

20. 35, ða *niðemestan* ic gebrenge æt ðam *hehstan* and ða *hehstan* æt ðam *niðemestan,* ðæt is, ðæt ic gebrenge *eaðmodnesse* on *heofonum* and ða *heofonlican* god æt ðam *eaðmedum,*—to which the Latin, *infima summis summa infimis* mutare gaudemus (II ii. 29). 50. 20, nan man for his *rice* ne cymð to *cræftum* and to *medemnesse;* ac for his *cræftum* and for his *medemnesse* he cymð to *rice* and to anweald,—the Latin has, *non virtutibus ex dignitatibus* sed ex *virtute dignitatibus* honor accedat (II vi. 11). 54. 33, ðæt ðæt *god* ne mæg beon wið ðæt *yfel* gemenged ne ðæt *yfel* wið ðæt *god;* 94. 20, ðonecan ðe *he* ðone *anweald* forlæt oððe se *anweald hine;* 134. 14, ðæt of ðam *mæstan gode* cumað ða *læssan god,* næs of ðam *læssan* ðæt *mæste;* 134. 15, ðe ma ðe seo *ea* mæg weorðan to *æwelme.* Ac se *æwelm* mæg weorðan to *ea,* and ðeah seo *ea* cymð eft to ðam *æwelme;* 134. 20, hwi ne miht ðu geðencan gif nan wuht *full* wære, ðonne nære *nan wuht wana,* and gif nan *wuht wana* wære ðonne nære *nan wuht full;* 196. 13, ðæs modes *tioð* eallne ðone *lichoman to him* and ðæs *lichoman* mettrumnes ne mæg ðæt *Mod* eallunga *to him* getion.

The special sentence structure underlying this figure gives it peculiar importance. The phrases or clauses are balanced in such a way that, were there no recurrence of the important words, emphasis would be given to the thought by the structure alone;

naturally, therefore, when to this is added the repetition of the leading words, the rhetorical force of the thought is further brought out, and the figure becomes one of the most telling in this category.

Gerber's [1] quotations very well illustrate the terseness and vigour of the figure in Latin literature; and in later literature it will be found to be equally effective, and used to as great an extent. Proverbs and epigrams are never more striking than when put in this form. Shakspere's "Better a witty fool than a foolish wit" (*T. N.* I. v. 39) and Christ's "The sabbath was made for man, and not man for the sabbath" (*Mark* ii. 27) illustrate the terseness and pithiness this figure gives in the expression of thought.

The figure, it will be noticed, occurs in A. H. only less frequently than Anaphora and Epiphora, but in W. H. it is rare and in B. H. does not exist. That it is rarely if ever found in the poetry may with tolerable safety be inferred from its not appearing once in *Beowulf.* The figures of repetition are all comparatively rare in the poetry, for, though the thought is frequently repeated, it is generally expressed in different words. From the formidable list of kennings collected by Dr. Bode and the other numerous synonyms existing in the poetic vocabulary, we gain some idea of the abundant means there were to avoid repetition of words. This figure with the others was, therefore, distinctly a devise of prose; that it was so sparingly used in the homilies would seem to indicate that it was not native but due to foreign influence, to which Ælfric, who has the greatest number of examples, was probably most susceptible.

CONCLUSION.

Broadly considered, there is nothing peculiarly distinctive in the tropes of Anglo-Saxon prose to give a special significance to this literature. So much is borrowed, either directly or indirectly, from foreign sources that the essentially native idea can hardly be distinguished from the foreign. The literature of

[1] II 212 f.

the learned classes, to which the homilists belonged, consisted of the *Vulgate* and the *Church Fathers.* These contained practically all the metaphorical ideas that we find in A. S. prose; those which seem most likely native are not of such a distinctly national character as to preclude their existence in another literature and their being borrowed, and adapted to the A. S. audience. Generally, the author emphasizes a trope which especially strikes off A. S. conditions and thus indicates the aptness of the idea, if not its originality.

The tropes are simple in their conception, and are used as they occur to the mind of the preacher. There is no studied or dramatic display, no climactic closing of a sentence with a metaphor, which writers of the eighteenth and nineteenth centuries have used with such fine effect; this can come only with a high degree of literary culture. The close of many of Burke's paragraphs are metaphors which sum up all that precedes in one forceful and comprehensive idea. This the A. S. metaphor never did.

Professor Earle remarks that "prose gets its inspiration from poetry—assimilates the characteristics of poetry." It is manifest from a comparison of the metaphors quoted above with those collected by Professor Gummere that the metaphors of prose and poetry are quite distinct. The metaphor of the poetry is in harmony with the spirit of the poetry; it is bold, picturesque, essentially Germanic. The metaphor of the prose, like the content of the prose, is borrowed, and, for the most part, has not been recast into such a mould as to have the virtue of even transformed thought. It has not been inspired by the metaphor of the poetry. In fact, we can hardly speak of the prose of the homilies as national at all; the temper of the Anglo-Saxon, as declared in even the essentially Christian poems, is almost absent from the prose. Wulfstan most nearly approaches it. Prose had not yet become the natural vehicle of expression for the most vital thoughts and feelings of the people; the men who wrote it were steeped in a foreign literature, their intellectual sympathies were ecclesiastical and Latin, not Germanic.

When we pass from tropes to figures, we enter upon conditions quite different from those hitherto considered. Tropes depend upon their content, figures upon their form to produce the intended rhetorical pleasure. In the former case the thought is strengthened by something external, a comparison expressed or implied, in the latter by the form or position of the words in which the thought is stated. Moreover, we find that the relations between prose and poetry are closer in the case of most of the figures. Poetry had practically no influence in creating the prose tropes, but many of the figures come directly from poetry, are the exclusive property of poetry. The figures of euphony, since they depend on the recurrence of sound to produce a rhythmical effect, are making use of a device which it is intended that only verse shall employ. Alliteration, the distinguishing feature of A. S. verse, rime, which was beginning to establish itself as the distinctive element of English poetic form, and assonance, which is closely related to rime, were all borrowed directly from the verse. The rhythm of prose was not understood by the A. S. writer; it is too subtle to be matched by the use of certain rhythmical devices of poetry. Hence Wulfstan writes prose which more resembles poetry, while Ælfric comes nearer the true prose rhythm by avoiding these extraneous devices. That there is more passion, intenser fervour in Wulfstan than in Ælfric is manifest, and these poetic figures are used to express it. Because prose had not reached its full development and had not come into the inheritance of later ages, Wulfstan resorted to expedients more familiar and of acknowledged propriety in verse to convey his passion. Wulfstan's style may be vigorous in these sermons, but it is not pure prose; it has that fault which corresponds to the scanned sentences of some pseudo-oratorical productions of the present day—though the comparison is unfair to Wulfstan.

On the other hand, the word-figures, which in A. S. literature are more frequent in prose than in poetry, are used by Ælfric more abundantly and with greater skill than by any of the other writers considered. The grammatical figures which mar much of the prose of B. H., he avoids to a considerable degree; the most important figures of this kind serve to express his thoughts with clearness and vigour. As in the other figures which are not exclusively poetic, Ælfric rises superior to the Blickling Homilist, Wulfstan, and the translator of *Boethius*, and further establishes his place as the best of the A. S. prose writers.

www.ingramcontent.com/pod-product-compliance
Lightning Source LLC
Chambersburg PA
CBHW030008030726
47499CB00008B/2957